001.64092
PRO

HEROES.COM

the names and faces behind the dot com era

by

LOUISE PRODDOW

Hodder & Stoughton

A MEMBER OF THE HODDER HEADLINE GROUP

Orders

Please contact Bookpoint Ltd, 78 Milton Park, Abingdon, Oxon OX14 4TD.
Telephone: (44) 01235 827720, Fax: (44) 01235 400454. Lines are open from 9.00am – 6.00pm
Monday to Saturday, with a 24 hour message answering service.
Email: orders@bookpoint.co.uk

British Library Cataloguing in Publication Data
A catalogue record for this title is available from The British Library

ISBN 0 340 78172 6

First published 2000
Impression number   10 9 8 7 6 5 4 3 2 1
Year 2005 2004 2003 2002 2001 2000

Photography   Jennifer Hands, Richard Branson by Thierry Boccon-Gibod

Typeset & Design   by **GYRO**
the technology agency

Printed in Italy for Hodder & Stoughton Educational, a division of Hodder Headline Plc, 338
Euston Road, London NW1 3BH by Printer Trento.

to

David and Alex

Acknowledgements

The Internet is not just about technology, it's about the individuals who are shaping the future. It is these dot com heroes that provided the inspiration for this book. Innovative and dynamic individuals who are doing things differently, with passion, with vision. Changing the way we work and play, breaking away from the corporate rules of the past. These are the people who sparked my ideas and helped me develop the business models that are featured in the book. A big Thank You to you all.

My work at Sun Microsystems means I network with many Internet pioneers – both in big business and start-ups – brainstorming ideas, developing, defining and implementing leading-edge marketing and Internet strategies. These highly talented people have given me a deep insight into the networked economy. A big thanks to all the companies, partners and agencies I have worked with. Special thanks to Shanker Trivedi and Darlene Yaplee at Sun for supporting such a personal project.

To Keith Roberts, Nigel Hopgood, Steve Raby, Leslie Stretch, Catherine Raymond, Martyn Lambert, Andy Thomas,, Andy Bush, Dave Thompson, Roy Chadowitz, Jim Hassell, Soren Jespersen, Jon Tutcher, Fiona Gallagher and Jean Gomes; our shared experiences and hours of discussions have been invaluable – thanks.

As with any good dot com idea, turning this into reality was only made possible through the hard work of a strong dynamic team. Richard Perry pulled the team together, researching, chasing and generally keeping everything on track. He was ably backed by Fiona Knowles, Nicola Beck and Rachel Knight who all had endless energy and enthusiasm.

Thanks to Sarah Walker, Mike Abbott and Nicholine Hayward with whom I shared the interviewing, ensuring we met the publishing deadlines and helped cope with the availability and diary pressures involved in a project of this scale. Credit goes to Jonathan Gabay who edited much of the copy.

The energy and passion of all the heroes could not have been captured without the stylish photography of Jennifer Hands and the art direction and design contribution of Jay Purcell. Thanks also go to Graham Dodridge and Gary Brine at Gyro and Philip Dodd at the ICA who supported the whole project.

And finally a special thanks to Tim Gregson-Williams at Hodder and Stoughton, the publishers, who brought the project to life. He greeted my initial ideas with amazing enthusiasm, ignited the project and provided continual encouragement.

Thanks to all the heroes of today. I hope their stories will inspire more people to embrace the Internet. To help make this happen, all the proceeds of the book will go to the Year of Promise for Internet-related community projects. Our first is the creation of an Internet café in Wales; a place for the youth to share ideas and get online to a new future. To all heroes of today and tomorrow, happy dot com-ming.

Contents

Chapter 3

Clicks & Mortar
Pioneers Going Beyond Traditional Boundaries

Chapter 4

B2B
Transforming Business-to-Business relationships

Foreword

by Paul Taylor

Heroes.com is about a new breed of individuals – the Internet entrepreneurs who are shaping the future of the digital or 'new economy'.

Internet entrepreneurs come in all shapes and sizes. Some are students or technology 'nerds', others come from the world of traditional business, while many have given up earlier careers as management consultants, accountants or lawyers to join the Internet revolution.

But it is what they share in common that defines these new age heroes. They are the 'prospectors' of this new gold rush – people of imagination and vision who are not afraid to take risks and challenge conventional wisdom. And like their Klondike counterparts, they are driven by a determination to succeed.

Unlike many of the business leaders in the old economy, they have either jettisoned or never been burdened with 'legacy' thinking and out-of-date business processes. They think 'out-of-the-box', believe that the Internet will enable most business activities to be done differently and believe that almost anything is possible – at least in terms of technology. They know that the Internet can be used not just to cut costs, streamline supply chains and improve business efficiency, but also to expand business horizons, reach out across the globe and grow new sources of revenues.

They also know that in the Internet economy David can challenge Goliath, that brand dominance in the physical world can be challenged on the Web and that the physical assets of traditional bricks-and-mortar companies can quickly become liabilities in a virtual world where time, speed and flexibility are vital.

They are committed to the vision of the Internet economy, to open standards and to customer power. They are the driving forces behind top websites like Yahoo, QXL and Amazon.

Some may well turn out to be the Rockerfellers and Morgans of this new business revolution; others will fade into obscurity after their 15 seconds of fame. But what is beyond doubt is that they are all helping to re-write the conventional rules of doing business and defining new business models for the future.

Reading about these entrepreneurs and their strategies for success in the dot com era provides inspiration and insight into how to be a successful individual. Perhaps for the first time, the emergence of Internet entrepreneurs has made business 'sexy' and 'cool'. Today businessmen can be heroes alongside our sportsmen, film stars and musicians.

In Bombay, Shanghai and Seoul as well as London, Helsinki and San Francisco, a new Internet-aware generation is growing up with a new set of role models. Today children aspire to be computer programmers, Web designers and Internet entrepreneurs as well as doctors, lawyers and politicians.

Many are attracted by the potential for huge financial rewards, but they also seek the lifestyle of this new breed of innovators who play by different rules in a dynamic fast moving world.

For years business leaders have battled against the image of industry, commerce and finance as 'worthy but boring'. Now, thanks to the disruptive technology of the Internet, this age-old stereotype may finally be consigned to the dustbin. The Internet, and the business entrepreneurs that are exploiting the opportunity it presents, are helping to redefine people's expectations and their ambitions.

This book gives valuable insights into how to start or remodel business strategies to take advantage of the new opportunities that the Internet and dot com era have created, and it highlights a fundamental truth – that success is based on strong personality and vision.

To succeed in the dot com age requires both determination and an ability to look past the obvious – to see over the hill. As one of the songs in South Pacific, the musical, notes: "If you don't have a dream, how are you going to have a dream come true?"

So welcome to the networked age, the dot com era.

There are many versions of the Internet story, but most people agree that, like many other developments involving computing, the Internet grew out of cold war rivalry. In 1957, the Soviet Union beat the US into space by launching the first Sputnik satellite. As part of its response, the US government set up the Defence Department's Advanced Research Projects Agency (ARPA) to develop new technologies.

By the mid 1960s, the US government had realised it had lots of extremely sensitive information stored electronically at ARPA and was concerned that the information could be vulnerable in the event of atomic war.

Defence chiefs reasoned that, if war broke out, networks would be more difficult to destroy than isolated supercomputers based in known scientific research establishments.

In 1969 Arpanet was set up linking four defence supercomputers – three in California and one in Nevada. The purpose of Arpanet was to evaluate how computers could be linked together using telephone lines, satellites and radio technology. This would enable computer scientists and engineers working on military contracts all over America to share expensive computers and other resources.

Almost as an after-thought, the researchers also developed a means of sending electronic messages, or 'email', as it became known, thereby turning the network into a new communications link.

In 1973 the embryonic Internet was extended to the UK and Norway using undersea telecommunications links. Meanwhile computer programmers developed a new networking protocol or standard called Transmission Control Protocol and Internet Protocol or TCP/IP which enabled every Arpanet computer to network with each other. TCP/IP remains one of the core technologies of the Internet today.

By 1979 the term Internet had begun to appear. But even in 1983 the Internet consisted of fewer than 500 'host' computers almost exclusively in American military laboratories and academic institutions. During the 1970s and 1980s other countries, including Britain, began expanding their own interconnecting networks while in the US responsibility for running the Internet 'backbone' of high speed data links was handed over to the National Science Foundation, which promotes science in America.

The NSFnet network originally linked five university supercomputers, but beginning in 1986 the network was expanded. By 1987 the Internet had grown to include 28,000 host computers at hundreds of different universities and research labs. Nevertheless, despite its obvious attractions in terms of providing universal connectivity, using the Internet was still a difficult and frustrating experience, and the Internet remained largely a cloistered world of academics and computer enthusiasts.

Several factors changed this for good.

First: During the late 1980s, while the Internet was growing in the academic world, a networking revolution of another sort was taking place outside academia. Businesses which had embraced the PC revolution began wiring their PCs together to share data and devices such as printers. These internal 'local area networks' did more than save money; they changed the way people worked. Internal email systems developed and people began using the networks to co-operate on projects.

Second: The falling price of PCs had made computer power affordable to home users, and modems had allowed them to be connected up over telephone lines to commercial 'online' services such as CompuServe and America Online, providing an early taste of electronic communications and commerce.

Third: In Geneva in 1992 Tim Berners-Lee, a British scientist working on the European CERN nuclear research project, developed a new easy-to-use way for exchanging information over the Internet using pages of graphics and 'hot-links' between words. His work became the basis for the first Mosaic browser software developed in the US by the University of Illinois and subsequently commercialised by Marc Andreesen at Netscape, the company set up by Jim Clark, the Silicon Valley entrepreneur and founder of Silicon Graphics.

Netscape launched the first version of its Navigator browser software in December 1994, it was an early licence of Sun Microsystems' Java software and became the first big Internet company to conduct an IPO (Initial Public Offering) in August 1995.

Netscape's success stung Microsoft into action and ultimately led to the Justice Department anti-trust suit against the Redmond, Washington-based software giant when Microsoft began bundling its rival Internet Explorer browser with its dominant Windows 95 desktop operating system.

Meanwhile with telecommunications deregulation gathering pace, the US government had been steadily relaxing its hold on the Internet allowing companies to use the Internet for the first time and privatising the Internet 'backbone' infrastructure. As restrictions were eased commercial use soared and by 1994 companies passed universities as the dominant users. A year later all remaining curbs on commercial use were lifted, and the National Science Foundation began to phase out the last direct federal subsidies for the network.

With the help of tools like Web browsers and the Java programming language, the Internet was transformed in just four years from an arcane system linking mostly academic institutions into a global transport system with 50m users. Today, that figure has swollen to perhaps 200m and estimates for the electronic commerce that it enables are pushed up almost weekly.

Within a few years most analysts expect the number of people with Internet access to pass 1bn representing what Craig Barrett, Intel's Chief Executive, has called "a brand new electronic continent".

The size of the potential marketplace explains why both dot com start-ups and their more traditional clicks & mortar rivals have been scrambling to build their Internet presence.

Among the first companies to capitalise upon the growth of Internet were the infrastructure companies like America OnLine, Yahoo and AltaVista.

Yahoo, the most successful of all the Internet portals and arguably the quintessential Internet stock, was founded by David Filo and Jerry Yang, two PhD students in Electrical Engineering at Stanford University. They started their Internet directory in April 1994 as a way to keep track of their personal interests on the Internet.

Meanwhile the race to build online stores was led by people like Jeff Bezos, the founder of amazon.com. Amazon's success shook up the booksellers market and helped pave the way for the thousands of e-tailers that now populate the Web.

Early online retailing initiatives focused on several core markets including travel, music, electronics and books and many observers questioned whether 'soft' goods, food or fashion items, would ever be sold over the Net. But today the success of a wide range of online retailers selling everything from cakes to cars has proved that there are no limits to what can be sold over the Web.

Among the biggest investors in consumer e-commerce have been the banks and financial institutions like Charles Schwab, now locked in fierce competition with upstart rivals like E-trade. However the Internet has also proved an effective vehicle for other sales models including auctions pioneered in the US by eBay and in the UK by QXL, the online auction house set up by Tim Jackson, an IT journalist turned Internet entrepreneur who now runs the Carlisle Group's European operations.

Other Internet entrepreneurs who have developed innovative new sales models include the founders of lastminute.com in the UK, Martha Lane Fox and Brent Hoberman and Brokat's founders in Germany whose online trading platform has enabled the development of new fixed and mobile financial services.

While Internet consumer e-commerce revenues still represent a small proportion of total retail sales, they are growing rapidly. This year business-to-consumer revenues in Western Europe alone are expected to total about $12bn according to IDC, the market research firm, and will double next year.

But it is the spectacular growth of business-to-business e-commerce revenues which has really caught investor's attention over the past 18 months. Even conservative estimates of the size of the B2B e-commerce market suggest it will grow to at least $1,500bn in 2004, up from $114bn in 1999 and virtually nothing two years ago.

While the B2B market may lack the glamour of the retail e-commerce market, the business opportunities and the innovation taking place are at least as significant.

For example, this year has seen a slew of announcements about the establishment of online exchanges in industries ranging from pharmaceuticals to autos and steel. These exchanges are designed to streamline the supply chain by bringing suppliers, buyers and partners together and in some sectors are expected to save tens of billions of dollars a year.

Other Internet entrepreneurs, like the founders of Inktomi, have focused on the provision of infrastructure services to the fast expanding universe of dot coms and their clicks & mortar rivals. Now they are being joined by a new set of infrastructure providers focused on the emerging mobile Internet – a market which some analysts believe could quickly dwarf fixed Internet access.

Durlacher, the research-led Internet investment bank, estimates that the European-led mobile commerce or m-commerce market could grow from Euros323, last year to Euros23bn by 2003. Such a prospect has hardware makers like Nokia, Ericsson and Psion as well as software developers and content providers all competing for a slice of this new segment of the network economy.

The provision of bandwidth itself is in a state of flux. Today, one strand of Qwest's US network can carry all North America's telecoms traffic and in a few years the same strand of glass fibre will be able to carry all the world's network traffic.

At home and in the office, broadband technologies like ADSL and cable modems will enable a whole new class of consumer and business services to be delivered over the Internet. Meanwhile in the mobile market the development of new broadband technologies will enable so-called third generation networks to deliver high value added services like video conferencing, rich Web pages and e-commerce services to consumers via palm-sized devices and smartphones.

The astonishing growth of the commercial Internet and network computing since the mid 1990s has highlighted the accuracy of "Metcalfe's Law" promulgated by Bob Metcalfe, the engineer who invented the Ethernet protocol. His 'law' states that the value of a network is proportional to the square of the number of nodes attached to it.

Meanwhile the number of 'nodes' is set to explode as more and more devices become Internet enabled and the PC becomes just one of the many devices used to access the Internet and its resources.

Less than a decade after the Internet first became a mass market phenomenon it is already clear that our world has changed for ever. Not only has the Internet and those who have pioneered its development changed our working lives, our leisure activities and the provision of both entertainment and education services are also undergoing far-reaching change. Even our political institutions and the fabric of government itself will be transformed by the Internet.

Within traditional industry and commerce, no company can afford to ignore the Internet today and perhaps the greatest boardroom challenge for old-style companies is how to respond to the dot com challenge. At least one option – that of doing nothing – should be ruled out. Not least because if you do not rise to the challenge, your competitor, or even a new entrant, will. Some analysts believe we are in a transition phase and that within perhaps as little as 10 years, all companies will be e-businesses, or they will not be in business at all.

Certainly the Internet places a premium on speed of change and flexibility, but it also requires companies to address issues like customer focus and marketing.

Many of the rules of doing business in the Internet age may have changed, but the prime directive – survival – has not. This book is about some of the people who have shaped the Internet age but it is also designed to provide the reader with valuable hints and tips on how to become one of the dot com heroes – how to thrive, not just survive in this new business environment.

Hopefully it provides ideas on how to be one of tomorrow's winners in this increasingly competitive, global economy. But most importantly, it sets out to show that there is a hero in us all...

Paul Taylor, May 2000

Introduction
by Louise Proddow

We are in the midst of a truly remarkable period, the Internet age, the era of the Net Economy.

A world that never sleeps – online trading 24 hours a day, global markets, an email culture of anytime, anyplace, anywhere. A technological world speeding faster by the day, a world in which the brave bloom and those just standing by are doomed.

This book takes a wide-angle lens look at the relentless heroes that are shaping the future. Their achievements will give you a lead in how you too can become a hero, harnessing your talent to enter the Net Economy.

From the mass media pioneers like Amazon and Excite, to heroes transforming traditional business like the FT and BBC; from the large corporate heroes like Sun and Cisco to the new entrepreneurs of Lastminute and Peoplesound. These are the heroes of the dot com age.

To confine these heroes to one set of criteria such as market dominance or wealth would be unjust, inappropriate, and inconsistent. From new 'clicks only' companies, to 'clicks & mortar' established business, from start-ups to blue chips, from individuals to artists, the heroes leading this vast dot com revolution are distinctively different, collectively making an incredible impact. As variant as chalk and cheese, they are truly the heroes of the moment.

There is no such thing as a typical Internet tycoon. These twenty, thirty, forty something and above heroes have deceptive appearances, moving beyond the stereotypical pinstriped businessman.

Our 21st century heroes, inventors of the Internet age, all have a professional, compulsive, entrepreneurial spirit. They demonstrate the ability to be unassailable managers as well as entrepreneurs, constantly innovating at every possible moment. Our heroes are the founders, the shapers and the risk takers.

These heroes are passionate about the Net Economy, it goes beyond their wealth and personal achievement. Highly talented, they have created a new style of business management.

In deciding on our selection, we could have chosen only the conspicuously successful, narrowing the search to captains of industry. Yet that would not do justice to the new dynamics of the dot com era. Compiling the list of heroes called for a mix of fact, educated opinion and networking across the digerati.

Many of the heroes are not just tied to companies or other individuals. By canvassing industry insiders, journalists, bankers, investors, analysts and more, we plucked some lesser-known heroes out of obscurity. We also aimed at promoting the diverse cross-section of those shaping this cyberfest. Although manifestly absent from the richest list, individually and collectively they too make a magnificent impact.

Louise Proddow

The primary aim of this book is to share with you the vision and passion of those heroes shaping the new Internet age, providing a starting point for ideas, observations, and predictions. It is people that underpin the dot com economy and I hope these will inspire you to become a dot com hero.

This is a time which raises many questions, many call it a new Net Economy. Faster time to market, the rise of the dot com business – Amazon, Excite, Lastminute – many people regard the change with fear. The Internet has changed everything.

Because of the scale and pace of the change many people are left with many questions, they want to know more about how they can harness the power of the Internet.

How can you and your company benefit from the Internet? How do you create a successful website? How do you turn your dot com idea into a reality? How do you ensure your established business remains competitive? How can you nurture your creativity online?

The interesting truth is that once you get close to those companies and individuals that are leading the dot com era you find they all share a common set of attitudes. Everyone featured in this book:

- Passionately embraces the dot com era
- Recognises the Internet changes everything and opens up new opportunities
- Rethinks how they do things; makes dot com central to their strategy/life
- Plays by new rules, more open, more flexible, more dynamic
- Acts in Internet time and makes things happen fast
- Redefines business models, spins off new online businesses
- Focuses completely on customers
- Uses technology as an enabler and a competitive weapon
- Builds a scalable, reliable dot com architecture
- Recognises the value of partnerships and outsourcing
- Focuses on their core competencies
- Lives for today and enjoys the momentum and buzz of the Internet

Some people have always played by their own rules, like David Bowie and Richard Branson. The Internet is the catalyst that has enabled a new breed of manager to redefine how to be successful. These individuals are inspirational, talking to them clarifies the simple truth of what matters, embracing the Internet with passion, being flexible, taking risks, building a scalable, reliable infrastructure and being obsessed with customer service.

The starting point for all those featured in the book is that they use the Internet to add a new creative spin to life, they open up new opportunities, invent new ways of doing business and make it happen with amazing speed.

The purpose of this book is to share with you these new rules and demystify the dot com era. To share with you the lessons and personal insights of the pioneers, capturing from them their advice and getting a bit closer to understanding them, what drives them, why and how they have been successful. There are some amazingly colourful and interesting people behind the dot com revolution, who are all too often ignored. This book hopes to reddress the balance.

From top tips for being successful to Internet predictions, from visions for the future to personal soundbites, from favourite sites to personal histories, the interviews really get to the heart of the Internet. With a breadth of names and personalities the book captures the softer values of the Internet age – the people who use the technology to make a difference. Although everyone is different the collective voice gives a clear message: these are exciting times, do not underestimate the effects of the Internet and act now to make it part of your life.

Louise Proddow, May 2000

HEROES.COM

People with Big ideas. People that make it happen.
People that are shaping the dot com age.

1.James Caldwell - Aisa, 2.Drew Kaza - BBC, 3.Phil Letts - Beenz, 4.Alexander Broich - BOL, 5.Kajsa Leander - boo, 6.Mark Suster - Build Online, 7.Chris Dedicoat - Cisco, 8.David Lethbridge - Confetti, 9.Michael Dell - Dell, 10.Rob Wilmot - Dixons Freeserve, 11.Mike Harris - Egg, 12.Jeremy Silver - EMI, 13.Julia Groves - Eventures, 14.Maxine Benson - Everywoman, 15.Evan Rudowski - Excite 16.John Browning - First Tuesday, 17.Michael Foster - FT, 18.Brian Greasley - Genie, 19.Terry Gilliam, 20.James Slavet - Guru, 21.Dominic Riley - Handbag, 22.Nigel Underwood - Hilton International, 23.Robert Proctor - Internet Exchange, 24.Julie Howell - Jooly's Joint, 25.Steve Bennett - jungle, 26.Brent Hoberman - Lastminute, 27.Bob Davis - Lycos, 28.Peter Kenyon - Manchester United, 29.Kim Polese - Marimba, 30.Ron Denis - West McLaren Mercedes

31.Rouzbeh Pirouz - mondus, 32.Ellen Hancock - Exodus, 33.Davina Lines - Netimperative, 34.Paul Barry-Walsh - NetStore, 35.Phil Brown - Nokia, 36.Ernesto Schmitt - Peoplesound, 37.Charles Fallon- Pets Pyjamas, 38.John Beaumont - Planet Online, 39.Larry Levy - Protégé, 40.Tim Jackson - QXL, 41.Trinny Woodall - Ready2Shop, 42.Rob Lewis - Silicon, 43.Bob Head - Smile, 44.Benjamin Cohen - Sojewish, 45.Rob Hersov - Sportal, 46.Scott McNealy - Sun, 47.Sandy Nairne - Tate Gallery, 48.Hugo Drayton - Hollinger Telegraph New Media 49.Carol Dukes -ThinkNatural, 50.Ian Stewart - Upmystreet, 51.Richard Spinks - Vavo, 52.Victor Chandler - Victor Chandler, 53.Richard Branson - Virgin, 54. Mylene Curtis - Virginbiznet, 55.Pete Goss - TeamPhilips, 56.David Bowie - BowieNet, 57.Jeff Bezos - Amazon, 58.Dan Thompson - 365, 59. Susannah Constantine - Ready2Shop, 60.Andrew Doe - Confetti

internet tycoons

The network-centric visionaries

Internet Tycoons
The network-centric visionaries

These are the people who have shaped the networked age, they have big ideas and their companies have grown into the big players who provide valuable technologies, products, services and leading edge dot com strategies. Amazon, Excite, Sun and Cisco all have grand ideas that shape future business models.

The Internet Tycoons, people like Jeff Bezos of Amazon, Robert Davis of Lycos and Scott McNealy of Sun, weren't the first to discover the Internet. The Internet, at least in its early incarnation, was a system for academics to share papers between universities. But they are the powerful people who recognised its business potential and opportunities and put it to work for them. They are the ones who started to develop the new dot com business models that shape today's Net Economy.

While other people were saying 'what is the Internet?', the visionaries were already embracing the Net at the core of their business strategies. While the world still thought in terms of mainframes and terminals, Scott McNealy at Sun was pioneering the concept of network computing and, in doing so, building the powerhouses that run today's Internet. While traditional bookstores were regarding the Internet with a mixture of feature and suspicion, Jeff Bezos at Amazon was embracing e-commerce with enthusiasm.

These Internet Tycoons have claimed mind as well as market share, recall as well as revenue. Excite is one of the world's leading search engines. Amazon is synonymous with 'e-commerce' on the Internet, Cisco the backbone. These are the individuals who consistently inspired the next generation of dot com heroes.

All this has come about because the Internet Tycoons share a unique set of characteristics. They had – and still have – the vision to see the bigger picture. They have never perceived the Internet as a technology network but as a business environment in its own right. Committed, determined and focused, these are the people with the courage to take risks, make investments and adopt single-minded strategies. The Internet Tycoons embrace change, rather than brace themselves for it.

Change, to an Internet Tycoon, brings opportunity. Constantly adapting, merging and forming partnerships forms a core part of their success. And whoever is first to initiate it is the one to stake the claim to a new territory. Culturally too, they are ahead of the competition. They might have grown into big corporate organisations, now with global infrastructures and thousands of staff, but they still share a refreshingly people-focused and enthusiastic culture. They have realised, as the rest of the world will soon too, that an organisation is run by people for people.

The impact the Internet Tycoons have made is immeasurable. In fact, they have made the Internet what it is today: an increasingly fast, well-engineered global network of accessible information, resources and services. By pioneering concepts, as well as services, they have brought the benefits of the Internet to millions of people. Millions of people's first experience of buying online is through Amazon, and Lycos has transformed the complexities of searching the Internet, taming the worldwide wasteland it once was.

The risks taken by the Internet Tycoons and the lessons learnt have become part of our technological heritage and a rich source of business advice. They were the first to make the Internet an integral part of their businesses, a platform for communications and a repository of resources. They were the first to appreciate the advantages of connecting partners and customers. Dell, for example, takes around 40% of the company's orders online, increasing customer satisfaction and reducing support costs, while streamlining the inventory for manufacturing efficiency.

They use the Net to deliver better service to customers and complement it with traditional modes of operations:

- They are passionate with a clear self belief.
- They are flexible, dynamic and challenge the status quo.
- They form strong management teams and strong business vision.
- They see everything in the future being connected to the Web.

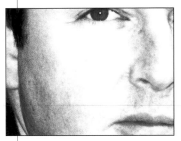
Chris Dedicoat – Cisco

We can learn from their universal admission that this is only the beginning. Every Internet Tycoon interviewed for this book agreed that the Internet will not only become more pervasive, but faster, more secure, more reliable. Doers as well as thinkers, they are the people who will make it happen. They will develop the new types of business, offer new services to customers, create the infrastructure, pioneer new concepts and approaches. And we can be confident that they will. As Robert Davis of Lycos himself says, "There's no time for complacency and relaxation".

If you want to know what the future holds, the Internet Tycoons are the ones to watch, they created the present and are still shaping the future.

Scott McNealy – Sun

Evan Rudowski – Excite

One of the Internet's most successful enterprises, Amazon offers 'the earth's biggest selection' of everything from books and music to toys and home products. Jeff Bezos, Amazon's founder, provides both the business expertise and the technology vision.

jeff bezos

The original hero

amazon.com

Jeffrey Preston Bezos is a man of many accolades. According to the *Sunday Times* Rich List, he has a wealth of £4.87bn. He was *Time* magazine's Person of the Year in 1999, the fourth youngest recipient of the title. Amazon is ranked as the number one online book retailer and the site itself has long been point of reference for anyone entering the e-commerce market.

From commerce-free zone to global shopping centre

But what Jeff will really be remembered for is his transformation of the Web from a largely commerce-free zone into a vibrant new world of content, commerce and community in 1994. Thanks to Jeff's vision, Amazon, named after the mighty, multi-faceted Amazon river, not only sells over 18m information-based products, from books to music but offers services that traditional networks just can't deliver: lower prices, a vast choice and extensive product information.

"You name it, Amazon will sell it"

As competitive websites put increasing pressure on Amazon's growth, the company is adding new categories as fast as it can and plans to double its offerings within a year. As Jeff told *Time* Magazine, "You name it, Amazon will sell it. Anything". His Coffeyville Distribution Centre, an 850,000 square foot warehouse has a free capacity of 90%, available for the ongoing e-commerce revolution.

Recent innovations include amazon.com Anywhere. Allowing remote access to the amazon.com site, Anywhere gives what Amazon's publicity describes as 'a safe shopping experience from Internet-enabled wireless devices'.

Jeff has always been fascinated by anything that could be revolutionised by computers. As a child he loved Star Trek. The garage was his laboratory. Enchanted by powerful vision, Walt Disney has long been one of his heroes. In fact, the fantasy, Utopian environment of Disneyworld, in which excitement is piled upon excitement in a never-ending array of wonder, shares much in common with that of the Amazon site. It could be said that the concept of stickiness began at Disneyworld.

Early riser, early adopter

After graduating from Princeton University with a major in electronic engineering and computer science, Jeff's early career was as a specialist in researching business opportunities in insurance, software and then the Internet. In 1994, at the age of 30, he found a site that measured Internet usage – and showed that usage was growing at 2,300%. It was, in Jeff's own words, a "wake up call".

Intrigued by this amazing growth, Jeff went to work. After creating a business model, he began to look for a product to sell. If it was to leverage the Internet's key strengths, it would have to be information based. And it had to be worth the customer's while. Jeff knew that "unless you create something with a huge value proposition for the customer, it would be easier for them to do it the old way". The logical answer was books. Highly databased, highly branded and straightforward to stock and distribute, books were perfect. Wholesalers even had CD-ROMs of titles, ready for Jeff to use.

Typically preferring to know rather than guess, Jeff took a crash course in the book business and got started. With three Sun workstations, a modest investment from family and friends and a 30% self-assessed chance of success, he and two friends got started. By June 1995 a rudimentary website had been created and friends and family were invited to give it a try. The next month the site opened to the public.

In less than a year Amazon was front page news on the Wall Street Journal and Jeff went to IPO offering $18 a share. But it had its detractors. Suffering heavy losses, the company was nicknamed amazon.org, as a non profit making organisation. Competitors, at last waking up to the opportunities, began e-commerce ventures of their own.

Automated efficiency from order to delivery

But today, despite a myriad of competitive offerings, Amazon is a byword for elegance and efficiency. The website's 'flow experience' ensures customers return again and again, and its complex processes have largely been automated. An international distribution network ensures fast, accurate order fulfilment. Even the warehouses are designed with streamlining in mind.

A banner at one of these warehouses provides the key, not only to the company's success, but its plans for the future. 'Our vision', it says, 'is to be the world's most customer-centric company, the place where people come to find and discover anything they might want to buy online'. Tellingly, the company's six core values are: customer obsession, ownership, bias for action, frugality, high hiring bar and innovation.

Customer heaven

What Jeff is aiming for is, in his own words, 'a nirvana state' of customer service. He advises his staff to "wake up every morning terrified, not of the competition, but of customers" and is sanguine about his competitors. Refusing to be drawn, he simply points out that Amazon has always been a customer – rather than competitor – obsessed company. He prefers to focus on listening to customers, innovating and continually improving their shopping experience. "I do not believe there is another company on the Internet that thinks about, talks about and asks about their customers as we do."

Moreover, Jeff disagrees with predictions of massive carnage among e-commerce retailers. He envisages a world "as complex and with as much variety as the physical world", in which there are not just a few winners but "tens of thousands".

Find it and buy it at amazon.com

But that doesn't mean that Jeff isn't prepared to fight for leadership. Indeed, with net losses of $350m in 1999 he can't afford to sit back. While the company holds stakes in up and coming e-commerce sites including drugstore.com, pets.com and gear.com, Jeff has high hopes for Amazon at the same time. As more customers come to his site he can offer lower prices. And they will come – because no other site does a better job in helping customers find and buy what they are looking for.

"Unless you create something with a huge value proposition for the customer, it would be easier for them to do it the old way."

"Wake up every morning terrified, not of the competition, but of customers."

Since he Co-founded
Sun in 1982, Chairman
and CEO, Scott McNealy
has been committed to
a vision of the networked
world and is leading
companies into the
networked economy
by delivering
services anytime,
anyplace, anywhere.

scott mcnealy

The dot in .com

sun.com

When did you first get involved in the Net?

When we founded Sun back in 1982, every employee had email from day one and our first product was Internet-ready with TCP/IP built in.

What is your greatest achievement?

Founding Sun (along with Bill Joy, Andy Bechtolsheim and Vinod Khosla) and having an impact on network computing – advancing the notion that programming interfaces should be open to everyone. We call it open network computing.

What are your three top tips for building an Internet business?

With anything on the Internet, you have to think in terms of billions of devices and millions of simultaneous users. Not only will everyone be connected, so will everything. If it has a digital or electrical heartbeat, it's going to link to the Net. So that's the model. That's what you have to build for. Second, you have to adopt a data centre mentality.

Continuous availability will be imperative. After all, the Internet never closes. And you have to design your infrastructure for rapid growth. In a word: scalability. You can't be competitive without it. Outsource anything that's not a core competency. Focus on what you do best and leave the rest to the experts.

Any advice for other start-ups?

It's more work to make a product or service simple, but it's worth it. First, because the consumer or end-user wants it that way – intuitive, easy to use. It shouldn't require a lot of instructions or training. Second, simplicity, in our experience, breeds reliability – which is another big plus from the user's point of view. Keep it simple and there's simply less to go wrong.

That's a big plus from the company's point of view as well.

Advice for a traditional business

It's time to dot com your business – and I don't mean simply selling products over the Net. If you use Internet standards throughout your organisation, it's going to be a whole lot easier to transact business with your suppliers and partners as well as your customers – to say nothing of your own employees.

Your vision of the Web's future

At Sun, we've been operating under the assumption that every man, woman, and child will be connected to the Net at all times. We're still a long way from that, worldwide, but we think it's the right assumption. Add to that anything with a digital or electrical heartbeat, as I said earlier.

I'll give you a couple of quick examples: when you set your alarm clock a half hour earlier, your coffee maker should know to brew the coffee sooner. And your car should be able to read your electronic calendar and give you directions to your next appointment without being asked.

Golden opportunities

Business has always been about building relationships. The Net is simply a way to build better ones – between companies and their suppliers, their partners, and their customers. One way to do that is with 'portal computing', which may prove to be the 'killer app' of the dot com era.

Portals enable you to provide information and services tailored to each group you do business with. It's a great way to build relationships and a sense of community.

How will you stay ahead?

By continuing to deliver reliable, scalable, platform-independent solutions. That's what companies need to thrive on the Net, and that's exactly what they get from Sun.

Any Net predictions?

The Net is about delivering services to anyone, anywhere, anytime, on just about anything. I've been saying that for several years now, and the vision is becoming a reality. In fact, in the next year or two, most Internet access will happen on something other than a PC – on smaller, simpler devices we can carry in our pockets. A lot of really great software is being created right now, but it's not being sold as a product, it's being offered as a service. That's going to change the basic business model moving forward.

Personal hero

Bill Joy – the Thomas Edison of the Internet. I didn't make that up, but I think it's an apt description. Bill designs software, hardware, networking – and makes it so even I can understand it, in principle at least.

Favourite sites

Any site that uses Sun systems, of course. That doesn't narrow it down much, does it?

Greatest thing about the Net

Anything you want is just a click away.

Worst thing

Anything you want is just a click away.

What inspires you?

The chance to make a difference. We started Sun with the idea that computers should be networked – that they should be able to talk to each other no matter who made them. Pretty wide-eyed, idealistic stuff, I know, but we've made some money and we've made a difference.

What should inspire others?

The same thing, I suppose. The chance to add value, to make a difference in people's lives.

Soundbite

"Kick butt and have fun." That may not sound terribly profound, but it seems to resonate with our employees. It's become our unofficial, internal tagline or motto. If you're not having fun, find another game to play – life is too short to do it any other way.

Any quirks or interesting facts?

Naw, I'm a family man. Having three kids is wild enough for me.

Other interests

I've been known to play a little ice hockey, a round of golf every now and then.

"Scalability. You can't be competitive without it."

Robert Davis, the fast-talking, fast-moving President and CEO of the Lycos portal, is a man who knows how to focus on the issues that matter. His commitment has turned Lycos from an initiative between a scientist, a salesman and a Venture Capitalist into a global presence.

bob davis

Finders keepers

lycos.com

Bob Davis knows what he wants and goes to any lengths to get it. He is President and CEO of Lycos, Inc., the portal that helps Internet users find precisely what they need.

Let up and you could lose your shirt

Several years ago, when Lycos was still in its infancy, Bob happened to be attending a management meeting in a local hotel. While there, he spotted a man wearing a T-shirt featuring the slogan: 'If you let up you lose'.

Enchanted, Bob wanted the t-shirt. He offered the man a Lycos t-shirt in exchange, however, the owner did not want to barter. Bob was determined and after a prolonged barrage of impassioned pleas, the t-shirt was his. Today the celebrated t-shirt is framed and hangs in his office as a reminder that persistence always prevails.

Such determination has stood Lycos in good stead. The company has developed from a $1.5m funded initiative between a scientist, a salesman and a Venture Capitalist, into a global media presence, with operations in 24 countries. Today Lycos is a multi-branded network, enjoying exceptional user growth and running four of the Internet's top 20 sites.

WWW = FFF (fast, fun, facile)

Bob attributes the company's success to a "fanatical devotion to customers". His unwavering dedication has helped set Lycos apart from a crowded and competitive market. Thanks to his efforts, Lycos makes the Internet fun, fast and facile.

Each highly individual site appeals to a specific user and market segmentation. "Keeping the customer happy is central to succeeding on the Internet," explains Bob. While there are more websites than Internet users, competition remains intense. In Bob's own words, "There's no time for complacency or relaxation".

People first

Bob feels, "Commitment is one of the keys to a successful Internet business". He advises traditional businesses to embrace the Internet now, instead of worrying how it cannibalises existing revenue. "You can't succeed unless you're committed. Don't be afraid." He also points out that, "Start-ups shouldn't overlook the essentials, like a strong management team as well as a strong vision and the ability to carry it out. Fund people, not ideas".

Commercially astute. Socially aware.

Bob's commitment also manifests itself as a strong sense of social responsibility. He declares, "The Web is the most dramatic social and industrial revolution the world has ever seen. It has transformed how we buy, communicate, capture information and socialise". Yet, Bob is appalled by the way the Web is used as a conduit for abuse – especially of young people. He is acutely aware of his duty to uphold the values of decency and protect the vulnerable.

"Keeping the customer happy is central to succeeding on the Internet," explains Bob. While there are more websites than Internet users, competition remains intense. In Bob's own words, "There's no time for complacency or relaxation".

Bob's dot com hero

As the Web becomes ever more pervasive, with access from a myriad of devices and a culture of globalisation, maintaining the Internet as a positive environment will become increasingly important. It is for that very reason that Bob names Ernie Allen, President of the National Center for Missing and Exploited Children, as his personal dot com hero. "Ernie has put the Web to use for a wonderful social purpose. He has harnessed its power to benefit those who may never experience the pleasures of surfing the Net."

A brighter future

With his customer-focused perspective, it is hardly surprising that Bob sees opportunities for Internet companies to create better, more efficient consumer experiences. Improving the status and operability of the Internet is Bob's personal, as well as commercial mission.

A keen Web user himself, he considers the Internet a great equaliser. "You can do anything, go anywhere, talk to anyone, all over the world."

To Bob, the Internet clearly has a greater significance and important role than just a communication channel. This is borne out by his choice of self-descriptive soundbite. "I made a difference in the world". It's the epithet of someone with a strong sense of community and a desire to enhance the Internet rather than just make money from it.

Head of the world's
leading direct computer
systems company,
Michael Dell is Dell.
His philosophy that
'Our Web strategy is
our company strategy'
has not only meant
a more efficient
inventory but lower
costs and better service
for customers.

michael dell

Online bespoke computer manufacturer

dell.com

Michael Dell is the founder of the world's leading direct computer systems company. It employs 33,200 people and sells its product and services in over 170 countries and territories around the globe. He is the pioneer of a bold concept – direct customer contact – this would not have been possible without the Web and has made Dell one of the most successful companies of the 1990s. "Our Web strategy is our company strategy", explains Michael. "Almost every one of our customers interacts with Dell in some way over the Web. It's the future of our company".

Receiving more than two million online visitors per week, Dell's Internet direct selling model moves more than $40m worth of computers every day. Dell is certainly practising what its CEO, Michael Dell, advocates "Go online, or go extinct".

At dell.com, customers may review, configure and price systems within Dell's entire product line, order systems online and track orders from manufacturing through to shipping. In addition to helping customers, Dell's infrastructure helps the company manage its own inventory.

Michael takes up the story: "I believe a fundamental shift in the definition of value is occurring. There used to be value around inventory; now there's value around information. Dell operates with about six days of inventory, whereas our competitors take about 60 days. Not only does this advantage allow us to deliver the latest technology to our customers faster, but because the value of components declines over time, we can provide a cost reduction to our customers".

Michael believes there's an inverse correlation between the quality of the information a company holds and the amount of inventory it needs. He explains, "Most businesses tie up a tremendous amount of assets anticipating things that may not actually happen. If they had a system that was customer demand driven, their assets would prove efficient. In other words, intellectual assets are replacing physical assets. Closed business systems are giving way to collaboration".

Practising what he preaches

Dell has integrated virtually all its business with the Internet. "Through the medium of dell.com we currently take about 40% of our orders online. This increases customer satisfaction and customer loyalty by reducing support costs. Turning our inventory around faster gives our suppliers a direct view into our demand trend so that they can assess their output to meet our exact requirements."

Top of the hits

In one quarter alone during mid-1999, dell.com handled 2.3m file downloads, 1.6m order status enquiries, 134,000 emails and 843,000 questions through the Online Knowledge Base system. Dell's Premier Page programme, with its personalised Internet pages, offers major corporations secure and tailored sales support via a standard Internet browser. Access can be password protected with tiered access privileges that provide customised support services. These may include tailored online order placement, inventory tracking and pricing as well as online links to Dell support representatives.

Dell's tips for the next generation heroes

Michael warns, "Simply establishing a website – putting a Web front-end on top of your company – is not going to create the efficiencies you need. You must re-evaluate how you're going to use information more efficiently and drive inefficiencies out of the system."

"Research has shown that the loyalty of online shoppers is related much more to the customer's experience than to traditional drivers such as price. As you look to harness the power of the Internet, focus on the online customer experience, thereby providing strong and loyal base. Think about featuring rich content; high-value commerce that moves transactions to the Web to reduce costs dramatically; and bringing communities together to create a network with shared interests."

Three steps to success

So how does Dell turn the casual surfer into a loyal customer? "The top two drivers of online loyalty are the quality of the customer experience and on-time delivery," answers Michael. "A company is vulnerable if this experience is not part of their differentiation.

"Dell focuses on three areas: building rich content, growing our commerce capabilities and establishing communities of suppliers and end users that share common interests."

"The first stage of content means providing compelling information. This is how we started our online operations in 1993, when we put our technical databases online for customers to access. It showed us the tremendous interest from our customers. Today Dell is recognised as an outstanding leader in online service and support."

"The next stage is commerce, which should be thought of as all transactions, not just buying goods over the Web. In fact, our first activity in this area had nothing to do with purchasing. It was simply order status. Customers would call and ask us to look up their order status. Manually that could be a time consuming process. Now we have an order status tool that links customers right into our system. It frees our people to become more productive and provide higher value-added activities. The estimated savings to our business through avoided status calls have exceeded $21m. This energised us to build an online system configuration that allows customers to build their own PC, which formed the foundation of our online sales."

"The final stage is developing an online community. At Dell, we've launched dell.net, which is our ISP and portal service. We are building two-way relationships over the Web with both our customers and our suppliers. For our small business customers we host Breakfast with Dell, an online forum to focus on 'hot' business issues'. We also have something called Dell Talk, a forum that brings users together to talk about their IT issues. Finally, we collaborate closely with our suppliers through valuechain.dell.com. This site for our top 50 suppliers provides exact information on our requirements and allows suppliers to see their quality results in real time."

Internet changing old rules

Michael concludes, "The Internet is having a profound impact on the global economy. We will continue to explore how best to use this technology to the advantage of our customers and to drive improvements in our business".

> "The top two drivers of online loyalty are the quality of the customer experience and on-time delivery."

Chris Dedicoat is VP and Managing Director of Cisco UK and Ireland; one of the Internet's greatest success stories. Chris has grown the UK business by 100% annually through his dedication to delivering global networked services.

When did you first get involved in the Net?

I was involved in the Internet in my previous jobs but to nothing like the extent I am at Cisco. Virtually everything at Cisco is done over the Internet.

What is your greatest achievement?

Growing the UK and Ireland business by 100% each year.

Key behind site

At Cisco, we have completely re-organised the way we do business, both internally and externally. We sell nearly all of our products online and the Cisco website – Cisco Connection Online – is the world's largest e-commerce site carrying out transactions to the value of $166m during the most recent quarter (three months) of the current financial year.

How is it unique?

We have an incredible customer focus. All the senior management team spend a good proportion of their time visiting customers. After all, a company is only as good as it is perceived to be by its customers.
We build a self-service culture which empowers the customer to the utmost.

What are your three top tips for building an Internet business?

1. Look at everything afresh.
2. An Internet business is not just having a website and selling products through this. A real Internet business (or e-business) re-organises everything through the innovative use of the Internet.
3. Choose something that will have high internal impact to help drive the necessary cultural changes.

chris dedicoat

Online connections

cisco.com

We have a virtual supply chain, customers can configure requirements and have them verified online. 80% of Cisco orders never touch any Cisco employee.

How did you secure finances?

Cisco UK and Ireland is part of Cisco Systems Inc, which is currently one of the largest companies in the world. We had revenues of £12.4bn last year, funding is not an issue.

Any advice for other start-ups?

Cisco was a start-up company not that long ago. My personal advice would be – don't ever give up.

Advice for a traditional business

To paraphrase Tony Blair – those who don't see the Internet as an opportunity will see it as a threat.

Your vision of the Web's future

Everything will be connected to the Web. You will be able to access the Internet in your car, through your mobile, through your TV, through your computer games and, of course, through your computer.

Golden opportunities

The Internet is changing the way we work, live, play and learn. The people and businesses who grasp this earliest will be the winners.

How will you stay ahead?

By maintaining a healthy paranoia about our competitors, by focusing ruthlessly on our customers and by keeping Cisco a great place to work.

Any Net predictions?

The Internet revolution has already started but it is quickly evolving to affect all areas of our lives in ways that we would not have dreamed of only a few years ago. All I can predict is that although I don't know exactly what the Net will be delivering in the future, it will get there fast!

Personal hero

Jack Welch, Chief Executive of General Electric, is my hero. I admire his ability to control an organisation that is so diverse and also successfully re-inventing it constantly, and John Chambers, CEO of Cisco. Under his leadership the company has grown to be one of the largest in the world.

Favourite sites

Cisco's internal e-learning education website.

Greatest thing about the Net

That it is a great leveller. Access to the Internet means that everybody, no matter where they live, has an equal opportunity.

Worst thing

I have to say that I cannot think of anything bad about the Internet, only that we must ensure it does not increase the divide between the haves and the have-nots.

What inspires you?

Being surrounded by hardworking, enthusiastic people who all have ideas, vision and the will to make it happen.

What should inspire others?

My advice to individuals is the same as to business – never give up and never be mediocre at anything you do.

Soundbite

Focused.

Any quirks or interesting facts?

I was advised by a previous employer that joining Cisco was a bad move as it was (then) a small company.

Other interests

Watching Aston Villa play and flying my Seneca, a twin-engine plane.

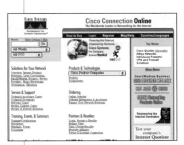

A thoroughly modern hero, Evan Rudowski, of the Excite portal, not only leaps before he looks, but never tries to predict the future beyond six months. He's certainly committed, though. Anyone who has seen the Grateful Dead in concert 60 times takes loyalty to a whole new level.

evan rudowski

Search guru

excite.co.uk

It's not Evan Rudowski's Masters degree in interactive technology that makes him a dot com hero. Nor his involvement with online services since 1986. It's his pure passion for the Net's verve and vitality.

Early in his career, Evan learned what makes an effective Net-centric business. Whilst at Newscorp in New York, he worked on an Internet effort called iguide. "Although iguide eventually crashed, it gave me a great grounding." Evan realised that nobody could predict how the Net would take off. Yet he committed himself to help develop the Internet's future. Evan moved away from print journalism to re-focus his career on new technologies. By 1996 he was ready to join Excite which had started a year earlier by a team of guys in their twenties.

One photocopier; countless dreams of success

"I was Excite's 45th employee. My role was to develop relationships with media companies. We had one photocopy machine and just enough PCs for everybody. Our rate of growth was remarkable. Today we have more than 2300 employees."

Evan's role in the company grew. "I become responsible for looking after the first acquisition that Excite ever made, a travel service called city.net. That led to my managing a good chunk of Excite's channels of vertical US-based content. Around two years ago, I moved to the London office to manage our European operations. The division has become one of the most successful online sites in Europe."

Following a belief – not the herd

Whilst Evan advocates building strong teams, he is suspicious of convention. "Successful people are flexible and dynamic. They adapt at a moment's notice. Any aspiring dot com hero should question assumptions and be entrepreneurial. Never be afraid to take risks."

Evan's philosophy runs deeply into the company's working ethos. "Excite has an expression: 'leap before you look'. Anyone building an Internet shouldn't wait for permission to try something. People who spend too much time analysing and not enough taking initiative end up left behind."

Does that mean future dot com heroes should avoid planning?

"By all means have a strategic position in place and business goal extending beyond six months. But, in terms of actual business activities and projects, never try to predict where the marketplace will go beyond six months. It's just too complicated."

The facts speak for themselves

Before any Internet business can forecast its long-term future, it has to 'sell' a Web idea to would-be capitalists. "Investors appreciate a professional business plan. In addition to defining the target market, you need to demonstrate a clear understanding of the market size. Explain where and how your customers spend their money. Consider how great a market share you can honestly expect to enjoy. In aiming at that goal, what would you be prepared to spend on marketing and what kind of revenues do you expect to generate?"

Changing perceptions at board-level

Evan advises traditional businesses wondering how best to develop an Internet service to entrust the Internet aspect of the business to non-conformist professionals. "They need to be true believers. Evangelists. Give them freedom and incentives to achieve success. If a traditional business can't accept a creative entrepreneurial culture within a large organisation, the directors may as well retire and play golf. They will never be successful on the Internet."

Always on

Evan's vision for the Internet is clear: "The Web will be always present and available whether you are at home or walking down the street." Evan is confident that people will interact with the Net in a far more sophisticated way than they do now. Technology will dramatically increase the Internet's usefulness and resources. Today we have to start-up the PC, then dial up and wait for connections. That's tedious. It's amazing that so many people are willing to accept it. It reminds me of what I love and hate most about the Net. On the positive side it allows people to stay in touch. Whilst on the downside it is slow and many sites are poorly designed. I just get so frustrated waiting for graphics and clicking on pages that go nowhere".

A broader horizon

Evan explains that as and when bandwidth is improved, the services and activities offered over the network will become more robust. "Soon everybody will have inexpensive broadband access. Following that, content and services will gain greater prominence. Dominant in our lives will be the brands of service providers who enrich us with incentives."

The best heroes are close to home

Evan doesn't have to search too far for his choice of dot com hero; George Bell, CEO of Excite. "He came from an established media company with no previous Internet experience. George has really helped the company articulate and evolve a corporate vision. Thanks to him, Excite has a culture of enthusiasm enjoyed by everyone associated with the company."

Newsworthy sites

Evan admits to a long-term addiction. "I am a news junkie. In fact, ever since I was old enough to read, I studied newspapers. My favourite news sites are MSNBC and cnn.com. They are both US-centric and so I can keep up with home news. I also like bbc.co.uk which provides high-quality news coverage of the UK and world at large."

An eclectic mix of pure energy

When not at work, Evan enjoys travel, photography and music. "I love The Grateful Dead. I have seen them in concert sixty times!" Unconventionality distinguishes both Evan and Excite from other Net success stories. "I would describe myself as hardworking, creative, friendly and yet serious. I get inspired by the chance to invent something new every day. No one should be constrained from what they want to do. At the end of the day, to reach full potential, everyone should be given the opportunity to find exactly what they're looking for."

If ever there was a resounding endorsement for Excite – Evan's must be it!

"Successful people are flexible and dynamic. They adapt at a moment's notice. Any aspiring dot com hero should question assumptions and be entrepreneurial. Never be afraid to take risks."

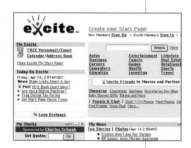

net entrepreneurs

Pushing the Internet into the new millennium

Net Entrepreneurs
Pushing the Internet into the new millennium

Business today is more relaxed, open shirts, open communications, open to new ideas.
Business is trendy and no longer filled with grey suits, we have a new breed of Net Entrepreneurs.
There have always been charismatic leaders in business, but they were confined behind
corporate walls.

Today the media is alive with stories of these Net Entrepreneurs, bringing to life a new attitude and style of management.
Net Entrepreneurs run many of the world's new breed of Internet start-ups that are now growing up into big business –
they personify the future. Brent Hoberman of Lastminute, Kajsa Leander from boo, Robert Proctor of Simply Internet,
Carol Dukes of ThinkNatural, and many more, all possess an energetic entrepreneurial spirit that has pushed them into
the limelight and gained them huge media profile.

They have media appeal, but it goes beyond this. They are less formal than traditional business leaders but they still
command respect by having heavyweight ideas and strong leadership skills. They have a self assurance, a real sense of
where they are heading. Fast decision makers, they respond well to the volative nature of the net economy and possess
an inner confidence to play by new rules.

The new rules of the new entrepreneurs are about new ways of doing business.

Almost without exception, the Net Entrepreneurs interviewed saw themselves putting their customers first. They are in
the business of providing a high quality service that customers not only need but actively enjoy, and, most importantly
delivering on their promises. They provide online services that add real value, that capture the very essence of the Net –
ideas that give customers more.

Net Entrepreneurs are business-people who also understand the power of marketing and technology. While they respect
the Internet's technological strengths, they see it as a channel for reaching customers. They didn't build the Internet, they
weren't around then. They haven't pioneered new technologies. But they have taken the Internet Tycoon's original vision
of the Net as the biggest marketplace in the world and created a place on it for themselves. They have harnessed the
power of the Web.

Their services began, not with a technological development, but with the identification of a need and a big idea. Take
Lastminute, founded by Brent Hoberman and Martha Lane Fox. Having always bought at the last minute, they recognised
an opportunity to link with late bargain suppliers. This would not only offer customers great value but help suppliers such
as hotels or airlines, sell products that would otherwise be left unsold.

Maxine Benson and Karen Gill likewise, while facing the challenge of setting up in business, recognised the need for a central place to exchange skills and information. It was from this insight that Everywoman was born. Pets Pyjamas' Charles Fallon created his website to complement rather than replace his catalogue service and, by doing so, offer customers a choice of channels. Richard Spinks was inspired to create Vavo, the seniors' portal, when he realised the benefits his father-in-law was enjoying from the Web.
In all cases, the driving force behind the Net Entrepreneurs is to provide a service that customers actually want. To them, speed of access, security, content, reliability are all vital, but most important is to enhance the customer's own experience. Customers, they appreciate, are looking for a service or a product. Charles Fallon, for example, talks of the 'customer-focused propositions' on his site.

Another factor that the Net Entrepreneurs have in common is the acknowledgement of the importance of teamwork and the vital contribution a quality management team can provide. They empower their employees to make decisions and draw on experienced consultants, partners and managers to bring in complementary skills. As business, rather than technology experts, they work with technology partners to deliver a secure, scalable architecture and they look after the content, the marketing, the positioning. They're not in awe of technology, but rather see it as an enabling tool to get the job done. Trinny Woodall from Ready2Shop, for example, is confident that the technology will be available, either from a third party or developed in-house, to help her reach her business goals. She meanwhile, will be concentrating on her job: to discover what women want and to give it to them.

While it was the early visionaries who built the Internet, it is the Net Entrepreneurs who are unlocking its potential by looking for new and better ways to satisfy customers. They are responsible for the rise in personalisation, for example. As Rob Lewis of Silicon points out, his job is to help IT professionals to cut through 'information overload' and provide a service personalised to the individual user based on their exact information requirements.

So what does the future hold for the Net Entrepreneurs? The answer is that whatever customers need tomorrow, they will provide it. The concepts of content, commerce and community have all been embraced – and further developed – by the Net Entrepreneurs and they will continue to do so.

The world of the new dot com start-ups may appear to have a youthful profile, but reality is that these companies are filled with experienced backers, consultants and employees. The Net Entrepreneurs draw on a broad base of experience and bring in others to support them. They know their own talents and do not try to step beyond this. They tend to set up a strong team behind them, often using their charisma and style to create celebrity status.

Behind the hype, all those interviewed in this section revealed strong vision, passion and business acumen that will continue to set the agenda for the dot com business arena.

Richard Spinks – Vavo

Andrew Doe – Confetti

Trinny Woodall – Ready2Shop

A dynamic combination of pace, innovation and creativity, Brent and Martha are the hearts as well as the faces of lastminute.com, which provides late bargains on everything from holidays and gifts to event tickets and restaurants.

brent hoberman
Quick getaway expert
lastminute.com

The best things come to those who wait until the right moment to grab an opportunity. Brent Hoberman and Martha Lane Fox did just that. Back in October 1998 they founded the highly successful lastminute.com. Like all great business ideas, their concept was simple: any company with a last-minute deal – whether it is for theatre tickets, hotel rooms, flights or holidays – advertised on the lastminute.com website. Customers seeking to treat themselves to something 'last-minute' hit the site – and the deal would be done.

Nobody understands the typical lastminute.com customer better than Brent who describes himself as 'the ultimate last-minute customer'.

"Having always bought at the last-minute I recognised some time ago an opportunity to link customers with late bargain suppliers. Such a service would offer customers great value. Likewise it would help suppliers, like a hotel group or airline, sell products that would otherwise be left unsold. It occurred to me that if I had a need for such a service so would others."

Born to conquer the Web
Brent's interest in the Internet began when he was about 13. At the time he lived in New York with his father. "I was excited by the global community aspect of the Web. Later, as a consultant at Spectrum Strategy Consultants, I worked more extensively on the Internet for companies like Cable & Wireless."

Early on, Brent could see the business potential of e-commerce. "From day one I loved the idea of buying goods over the Internet. At that point I couldn't find anything on the Web that I wanted to buy, yet I could recognise a compelling business case for Internet transactions. In my eyes, once the Web as a medium had attracted a sufficient mass of people, it was the place to make money."

Right from the launch – all systems were go!
"After three years I left Spectrum to join BT LineOne, the Internet Service Provider (ISP) set up with News International and United News. There I held the role of Business Development Executive, focusing mainly on e-commerce. Then I moved on to help start-up QXL. It was a fantastic experience. I was in at the beginning, even before there were any customers. I stayed for four months and then left to set up Lastminute."

It took Brent and his Co-founder Martha Lane Fox just eight months to launch the Lastminute website, "In March 1998 we wrote the business plan. Within a month we raised £600,000 from Venture Capitalists. Gaining early credibility with serious brand names was a huge advantage."

Between June to September Martha and I prepared the site for business. This involved building the technology infrastructure, getting suppliers on-board and putting delivery mechanisms into place. "Initially we launched a beta site. It didn't work very well," admits Brent. "Fortunately the concept was compelling enough for people to get excited. We improved the technology as we went along. Since we've started running on Sun systems there has been a noticeable improvement in site uptime and download speeds. We are now better geared to cope with peak traffic."

"From day one I loved the idea of buying goods over the Internet. At that point I couldn't find anything on the Web that I wanted to buy, yet I could recognise a compelling business case for Internet transactions. In my eyes, once the Web as a medium had attracted a sufficient mass of people, it was the place to make money."

Carving out their own market

The business has been phenomenally successful. In terms of sales, Lastminute is growing by an impressive 30% to 40%, month on month. In fact, every month it achieves over 10m page views. In Europe over 600,000 people have signed up for weekly email. Unusually, there is no US equivalent.

Financial success is obviously a major achievement. And what else? "A number of things", explains Brent. "Part of the fun is when the people working for us are excited by what they are doing. It helps them to discover new capabilities. Delighting customers and suppliers also gives us a buzz. I love to hear about a hotel that puts up 100 rooms and sells out within a few hours. The typical reaction is 'how did you do that?' Fulfilling a unique function within the marketplace is very exciting, especially when it's recognised," adds Brent.

Staying on top

Keeping ahead of the competition is vital. "It's all to do with pace, innovation and creativity. We have to keep going at this rate of change. Thanks to the culture at Lastminute we can. Martha and I are right in the thick of things. We don't have separate offices and we don't have egos. It all helps keep the company young and creative."

"Scale is also important. We're building what I'd like to think of as a global 'Lastminute' marketplace," says Brent. "Maintaining our lead calls for keeping our brand position, watching funding, recruiting the best people and nurturing the best relationships. Top marketing and great technology is what's so great about this business. It's not just about linking into a simple database like many other Web businesses, it's more to do with being ahead of the game with developments like digital TV and WAP phones."

People count

"Our team numbers more than 200 people. If you go around and consult all the managers, you'll get nothing done. For example, we were trying to get a voucher product live. Normally an idea should be approved by several departments. Yet I've discovered that when too many departments are involved, virtually any idea gets blocked. After all, not everyone is an entrepreneur. We're lucky to have people who can overcome problems. I'm really thrilled that we've got people around us who are truly entrepreneurial both in thought and spirit."

A natural entrepreneur

It's fascinating to work out the qualities that make someone an Internet entrepreneur. Brent says, "I think it's possibly down to my obsessive nature that I tend to throw myself into things. In the past, I haven't enjoyed jobs that lacked challenge or didn't encourage me to invest my energies".

A terrific outlook

Brent sees the Internet continually improving. "The Internet is already getting easier and faster to use. It's becoming a more pervasive part of our lives. On the downside today's Web technology is often too visible. It's an issue affecting many major sites. The key is to invest right from the start, in the best qualified technical people as well as most robust equipment."

The simplicity of lastminute.com has captured peoples' imaginations. The runaway success of the site has already made it a market leader. As for the future, Brent predicts running a truly global brand. "Working at this pace is exhausting, and I wouldn't recommend it forever – but for the moment it's great!"

However hectic the pace, should Brent decide to take a short break he could always book one – Lastminute.

"In March 1998 we wrote the business plan. Within a month we raised £600,000 from Venture Capitalists. Gaining early credibility with serious brand names was a huge advantage."

Inspired by his
father-in-law's enjoyment
of the Internet, Richard
Spinks created Vavo,
the over 45's portal that
not only gives older
people a voice but helps
them make a difference
to the world.

richard spinks

Redefining the Internet generation

vavo.com

Spotting the Web gap in the older market was easy for Richard Spinks, Managing Director of vavo.com. "The idea of providing an older generation portal struck me when my father-in-law Len, then aged 75, became a widower. Overnight he turned into an introvert person. He moved into our house until he was able to return to his own home.

"I had some computers lying around the house. So I thought 'bingo!' The family could introduce Len to the Web. Frankly, I was concerned whether at his age he could learn to use the Web, let alone turn the computer on. But he proved me wrong. He brought out a notebook in which he wrote, step 1 – press the button. He went through each stage. By the end of the week he was playing bridge on the Web."

The eureka moment

"Then one evening, around four in the morning, I heard a 'thump' from downstairs. My wife asked, 'What's that downstairs, a burglar or something?' I went to look. It was Len. He had fallen asleep by the computer. He had learnt to use a chat-room on his own and was talking to a lady in the States. Her husband had left her with three kids. He offered advice and support as to how to handle the situation."

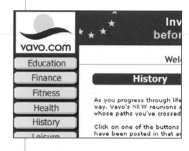

"It was fantastic. This guy who couldn't even work a washing machine, was using the Web to offer global advice. I knew that night that people like Len deserved their own place on the Web comprising a community of like-minded people, rich in life experiences."

Understanding the market

Richard discovered that apart from one US player – thirdage.com – run by a lady called Mary Fairlong, there was nothing substantial on the Web for the older surfer. He wanted his site to be bigger, better and more targeted than anything offered over the pond. That would call for careful listening to his prospective customer base.

Richard advertised in *Private Eye* magazine for 100 older people interested in joining a focus group about the Web. This was vital. "Aged 33, I didn't really know what they wanted from the Web. To my amazement, I got 974 replies. They ranged from, 'what the hell do you want?' to 'I'm really into the Net and this is what I would really want from a site'."

"This motivated me to seek funding. Before vavo.com I was number three in Lycos-Bertelsmann, responsible for building the traffic and the revenues on really significant levels. I have extremely strong relationships and contacts throughout the industry. I called a friend, explained the market gap and the potential of a site aimed at older people on the Web. He replied, 'Great OK'. I was ready to move. I knew where I was heading."

Widening Vavo's services

"We have just raised £10m, not through Venture Capital. We wouldn't touch VC. Instead a very good valuation of our business allows us to get cash and extend our product services. We aim to build services that will dominate our market. We will go head-to-head in price comparisons with companies who claim to offer good deals to the older generation."

Spinning money from the Web

Traditionally community sites are very broad based, including the topic areas that people build their home pages around. So advertising isn't that targeted. Vavo.com is different. Highly targeted people aged over 45 actively choose vavo.com as their preferred site of access and destination. Within the first year of being online their advertising inventory was all but sold out.

The traffic figures for Vavo show that in the first seven months, Richard attracted over 1 million older aged, discerning people to the site. "Vavo has grown organically in the community by word of mouth. In the first few months I spent between 6,000 and 10,000 bucks on advertising. A significant part of our future budget – a seven-figure sum – will be on PR."

What's the next big thing in the Web?

"I could be boring and say 'WAP' or mobile communications or convergence. I think the real change has to do with social matters rather than technological issues. Potentially, within six years, UK pensioners will vote at home via the Web."

Richard's advice for future dot com heroes

"Before there is even an online service, listen to your customer. If you want to run sites for say, pet owners, don't assume that just because you own a dog, you are the archetypal pet owning surfer. Ask for views from people who own snakes or maybe hamsters. Everyone talks about doing this sort of thing. Few do. Most go ahead and build sites. If surfers don't like the results, tough."

"Always offer feed back to your online customers within 24 hours. We try and answer within the hour. Thirdly, hand over the decision of site content to the people who are going to use it. Vavo has gone beyond attaining loyalty. We have earned gratitude from our community. Next, mirror your customers' wishes. Sure get your site to market fast, but encourage feedback. That's the bottom line: be brave and face the punters."

Who is your current dot com hero?

Richard's choice of dot com hero is Bill Gates. "He comes under a lot of pressure and flack. Yet has made it possible for anybody to take advantage of the Internet. In fact Microsoft devised a manual for how to build a website for someone aged over sixty."

Richard plans vavo.com to facilitate social change on a global scale. He would like to "wake up some of the younger people" in his age group to the fact they will also grow old. "I want to see the British government and others listen to Vavo members. Only six months ago, many Vavo members would not have had a global voice. Now they can organise themselves and discuss issues in large enough numbers to make a difference in their own lifetime. That is my main reason for constructing Vavo."

It's a worthy goal. It's a huge market. Bravo, Vavo!

Richard discovered that apart from one US player – thirdage.com – run by a lady called Mary Fairlong, there was nothing substantial on the Web for the older surfer. He wanted his site to be bigger, better and more targeted than anything offered over the pond.

Young, on-the ball and highly astute, Ernesto Schmitt, a 28-year-old, US-born, German-Uruguayan is the President and Chairman of peoplesound.com, one of the year's hot tickets in the UK Net community. The site provides a revolutionary platform for new talent in rock and popular music.

With European expansion in mind, Ernesto aims for Peoplesound to go head-to-head with the major US-based players in the delivery of digitally downloaded music. "We're not in competition with the music industry, we're complementary," explains Ernesto. "We provide musicians with a platform for their creativity in an environment that allows freedom of expression. Good musicians who don't normally get a hearing from major record companies can reach a global audience. Likewise we offer customers a choice of musical genre from any easily accessible site."

Re-shaping the future

According to Ernesto the Web is driving down prices and forcing companies with traditional channels to re-think sales strategies. "The Net is revolutionising how we do business. Look how insurance selling moved from door-to-door to becoming phone-based. Today no one would launch an insurance product other than online. This new approach to consumer selling is making us all think differently. Sites like Peoplesound offer virtually one-to-one niche marketing. My site can capture what customers like and deliver those needs. In return customers simply log on, pump in their ID and back comes the choice of acts that exactly match their tastes."

The music mogul believes that the Web can teach a few well-timed lessons to post 20th-century corporations. "Narrowcast retailing has arrived. Soon major high street retailers will offer customers what they want, rather than whatever happens to be on sale that season. Best of all, because the transaction is over the Net, costs are lower than in a bricks and mortar environment."

Top of the tips

Ernesto is convinced that his experience in turning Peoplesound into a Net market leader in less than nine months can help other budding dot com heroes. "First get your content right. By having in place what customers want they enjoy being part of it. Then it's all about quick access to information. Your site should feature a very fast, very clever search machine. In Peoplesound's case, we developed our own. After all we can't expect customers to wait half a minute for basic information, then longer still whilst checking out what is on offer."

Ernesto's next tip – think big. "To get noticed and ultimately survive, be big and bold on the Net. Millions of dollars are spent creating standout content and promoting websites. Aim to be in the major league."

Taking a leaf from Ernesto's own business model

In late 1998 Ernesto was a business consultant working on a large music industry merger. He became aware of new media's potential to change the face of popular entertainment.

Ernesto's next tip – think big. "To get noticed and ultimately survive, be big and bold on the Net. Millions of dollars are spent creating standout content and promoting websites. Aim to be in the major league."

Between January and March 1999 Ernesto assembled a team to put a 150-page business plan into action. It comprised of a bright management team – including some grey-haired experience from CompuServe to fill the job of Chief Operating Officer.

Drawing on his intimate knowledge of consultancy, Ernesto knew what investors wanted from a start-up. "People need to be confident that you understand an industry rather than dictate to it," explains Ernesto. He backed his proposal with detailed analysis (another tip – for budding dot com heroes seeking investment). By July 1998, peoplesound.com was launched and the rest, as they say, is history. Or perhaps, more apt for this particular start-up, the best is yet to come.

Uniting the world through music
Ernesto is set to roll out Peoplesound throughout continental Europe. Expect to see Peoplesound sites in France, Germany, Spain and Italy; all in local languages – and a team across Europe of 90-plus peoplesound.com people.

Ernesto's Internet vision
In these days of rapid technology change, nothing is too fanciful. Within ten years Ernesto foresees a super chip that will drive entertainment throughout the home. "Technology will recognise your mood when you get home and select the appropriate music or other form of entertainment to match." Dick Tracy wristwatch territory – who knows?

Ernesto recognises that WAP (Wireless Application Protocol) technology – currently all the rage – will herald breakthroughs in the ability of mobile phones to download digital quality music over the Internet. Net-exclusive radio stations will adapt WAP technology to receive CD-quality broadcasts.

Revolutionaries rule the Web
Ask Ernesto to name his choice of dot com heroes and the first that spring into mind are the Yahoo! Finance and BBC News websites. Why? "Great functionality!" he exclaims. "The Net is a very unforgiving place to sites that don't react in milliseconds to customer needs."

Heroes from an earlier age also inspire Ernesto. He admires Fidel Castro and Che Guevera. On his desk is a picture of the revolutionary partners and on it is the legend – We're at War. It's a daily reminder to Ernesto that for him business is a constant battle with a never-ending imperative to deliver appropriate customer benefits and improve services.

Long live the revolution!

"Technology will recognise your mood when you get home and select the appropriate music or other form of entertainment to match."

Davina Lines, founder and Commercial Director of netimperative.com, advises traditional businesses not to 'rest on their laurels' whilst she will be 'listening, leading and evolving'.

davina lines

Insider trader

netimperative.com

When did you first get involved in the Net?

By being part of the founding launch team of *New Media Age*, a weekly business magazine for marketers who work in the Internet space when the entire industry could fit into one wine bar with room to dance (June '95). I was responsible for setting up the commercial side of the New Media Group, launching a number of industry events, a creative magazine and two online properties.

What is your greatest achievement?

Taking netimperative.com from a piece of paper to launch within three months with my two fellow partners, Felicia Jackson and Bryan Smith and a small team of highly skilled journalists.

Key behind site

Understanding the needs of our audience of Internet professionals by providing an environment to inform, communicate and transact.

How is it unique?

Not only is it a time efficient method of gaining localised industry information in a format relevant to the specific user's needs, giving them choice but it also provides a forum to realise your business potential.

What are your three top tips for building an Internet business?

Be smart.
Be fast.
Be flexible.

How did you secure finances?

Passion, hard work and contacts.

Any advice for other start-ups?

Clearly define your brand world and end game at the very beginning and continually refer back to it. Build an asset base, as the mistake most dot coms make is to build a brand around a business model that can be easily copied.

Advice for a traditional business

Don't rest on your laurels!

Your vision of the Web's future

Integration in everyone's daily lives through a multitude of channels – the PC at work, the PDA on the train, the mobile phone on the street, the TV at home.

Golden opportunities

Establishing a trusted brand online before the top tier in each sector is saturated. Existing brand names potentially have an advantage here, but not for long.

How will you stay ahead?
By listening, leading and evolving.

Any Net predictions?
Exponential growth over the next couple of years in multichannel Internet penetration both in the B2B and the B2C sector.

Personal hero
Carol Dukes – founder, thinknatural.com, who never fails to achieve, always gets great coverage whilst maintaining her modesty and is professional at all times.

Favourite sites
As a consumer – formula1.com as I am a huge fan of Ferrari. As a businesswoman – our own site netimperative.com

Greatest thing about the Net
The infinite possibilities.

Worst thing
The vastness – the industry needs to make it more accessible and filtered to the consumer or business user's needs.

What inspires you?
Being around so much talent.

What should inspire others?
The wealth of opportunity and creativity within the Internet industry.

Soundbite
"The best things in life are free."

Any quirks or interesting facts?
I change my hair colour with my mood, always have an opinion and am never shy in coming forward.

Other interests
Formula One ranks very highly but actually it's people – I find them fascinating, amazing and frightening all at the same time.

"The best
things in life
are free."

Bringing sports passion online with Sportal, Rob Hersov, CEO and founder, is a man with a strong vision and, with speed, strategy and commitment, epitomises the successful athlete.

When did you first get involved in the Net?
July 1998 when I launched my own Net company, Sportal.

What is your greatest achievement?
Building a 200-person operation in nine months, in 18 countries.

Key behind site
A long-term focus, a scalable model and a network approach to the complex international market.

How is it unique?
It is sports passion online.

What are your three top tips for building an Internet business?
Be decisive and move fast. Have a long-term view. Hire the best.

Your vision of the Web's future
Everyone in the world – connected!

Golden opportunities
Working from golden beaches in sunny places.

How will you stay ahead?
Focus, speed, commitment and funding.

Any Net predictions?
Within five years, everyone in the world will be connected.

Personal hero
My wife.

Favourite sites
theonion.com, FT.com, sportal.com

Greatest thing about the Net
Sending jokes to friends.

rob hersov
Sports passion online
sportal.com

How did you secure finances?
Firstly from friends and contacts ($7m), then from Venture Capitalists and then from Strategic Partners ($75m).

Any advice for other start-ups?
Hire people who have done it before and think global.

Advice for a traditional business
Embrace new technologies and make sure the CEO understands.

Worst thing
Dialling in from remote places.

What inspires you
A revolution is taking place and I am part of it.

What should inspire others?
The opportunity to take part and make a difference.

Soundbite
To infinity and beyond!

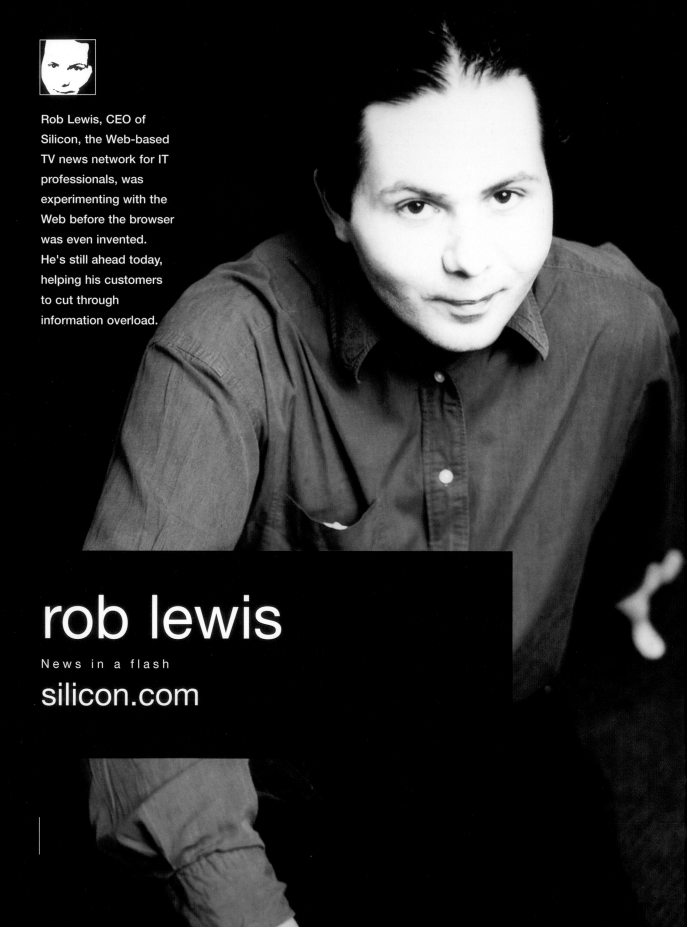

Rob Lewis, CEO of
Silicon, the Web-based
TV news network for IT
professionals, was
experimenting with the
Web before the browser
was even invented.
He's still ahead today,
helping his customers
to cut through
information overload.

rob lewis

News in a flash

silicon.com

When did you first get involved in the Net?

Since the early '90s – we were experimenting with the Web before the browser had even been invented

What is your greatest achievement?

Persuading private individuals to invest the initial money we needed to kick off the silicon.com project – at the time (back in 1997) the Internet seemed like a risky, wild frontier and there certainly were no VCs falling over themselves to give you their millions!

Key behind site

We provide a dedicated TV news network for IT professionals. Unlike most of the Web it is personalised to the individual user based on their exact information requirements. Personalisation is the key to the future of the Web – publishers can then genuinely use the Web for what it's good for.

How is it unique?

It's richly personalised and provides desktop access to TV interviews with the top gurus and personalities in the IT industry – enabling IT professionals to cut through the information overload caused by the 29 magazines they receive each month! Research shows almost all traditional IT magazines end up in the bin, unread.

What are your three top tips for building an Internet business?

1. Use the Web for what its good for.
2. Choose a memorable and Internet-friendly brand and URL.
3. Only bother if you have a sustainable business model.

How did you secure finances?

Initially from private individuals who saw the vision and agreed that the future of business-to-business publishing must be the Web. The advantages over paper publishing are staggering. The Web is faster, real time and personalised – it can deliver business TV on demand at the desktop for the first time. This initial capital enabled us to build a cash-positive and fast-growing business and also create a well known successful product and brand. After this initial success, silicon.com won a further round of European investment from Amadeus, Schroders, Dresdner Kleinwort Benson, Gilde and Deutsche Telekom. This is being used to set up a string of localised editions of silicon.com across Europe and elsewhere worldwide.

Any advice for other start-ups

Don't build a business for the sake of it – there's too many 'me-toos' around as it is. What matters is being first and being number one. Excellent execution also helps – you can have the best business plan in the world but if you can't deliver on it effectively you don't have much hope.

Advice for a traditional business

If you're a CEO who has responsibility for an old world and a new world business you'll probably spend most of your time in the old world business because it will be so much larger in revenue terms. The result? You'll lose the virtual war and the business will slowly but surely disappear to cunning up-starts. So how do you avoid this? Split the business in two – if not legally at least from a management perspective.

Don't be afraid of cannibalising your existing business. What you're actually doing is successfully maintaining a business relationship as your customer migrates from an old way of doing business to a new method. This is something to be proud of, not afraid of. Allow competition between the new and old businesses – if you don't compete with yourself you'll soon be competing with someone with a few million pounds of VC money behind them.

Your vision of the Web's future

The future will come from genuine Web and WAP integration: a world in which a user seamlessly moves from a personalised Web-based application to a mobile environment. In the longer term, the Web and Internet technologies will be omnipresent and transparent in our homes and workplace.

Golden opportunities

The biggest opportunities are in business-to-business. In ten years this could be up to 90% of the Internet in value terms. But to date the majority of the investment has been in consumer Internet. High-speed desktop Internet access in the workplace won't be threatened in the same way as consumer Internet is by digital TV, Playstation3 and so on. So the smart people and the cunning investors are looking for the B2B opportunities where user relationships, e-commerce and information value is of a higher order than we have seen in the traditional B2C arena. If you're thinking of setting up a brand new B2C website, think again.

How will you stay ahead?

The only way to stay ahead is to always presume you are behind.

Any Net predictions?

A huge reduction in valuations of B2C Internet dot com businesses when the B2B Web businesses IPO.

Personal hero

Not saying – as she's already too big-headed.

Favourite sites

FT.com for trying to make business news sexy. Ukinvest.com for giving me market news ahead of better known American sites. Oh, and for a great share price, Java app. that I use every day!

Greatest thing about the Net

Nobody knows what will happen this time next year. A day is a long time in the Internet. You have to act fast on every opportunity.

Worst thing

Everyone has to work so hard they'll be dead before they IPO!

What inspires you?

The team at silicon.com. In traditional business you have to spend most of your time trying to motivate people to even care. Here there's so much enthusiasm it can be overwhelming.

What should inspire others?

Using the Web for what its good for – personalisation, real-time delivery of information, accurately delivered demographic-specific advertising. Too many people do the Internet thing because they feel they ought to – not because they actually have a good idea.

Soundbite

Hopefully the *Sunday Times* headline, "Pony-tailed online TV boss to make fortune in £800m float" (joke). More seriously, as one colleague once said, "like every Gemini he never finishes anything he starts". In this game you hopefully never finish – after all, that means you've gone bust! If you're successful you'll continue the journey forward forever. The moment you stand still, you should say goodbye.

Other interests

I started the millennium experiencing cultures of the third world. No electricity, no computers, no potential Y2K nightmare. But I'd go back any day. It's important to remember and see the rest of the planet. Sadly, too busy to go very often.

> "The only way to stay ahead is always to assume you are behind."

Ready2Shop, founded by
Trinny Woodall and
Susannah Constantine,
has the best of both
worlds – the security of
a sound business
proposition plus the
satisfaction of helping
women make the best
shopping choices.

trinny woodall &
susannah constantine

Cybergirl's dream
ready2shop.com

A site for sore eyes

'Melons and fried eggs' doesn't suggest an appealing menu course, except perhaps at an exotic wedding, yet Susannah 'Melons' Constantine and Trinny 'Fried Eggs' Woodall hail as one of the most exciting partnerships to hit the Internet in years.

Trinny and Susannah, joint Chairmen and Co-founders of Ready2Shop first hit the headlines, so to speak, with their Ready to Wear column in the *Daily Telegraph*. Down to earth, with a wedge-booted foot firmly set in the real world, Ready to Wear soon became every girl's 'must-have' wardrobe accessory.

The women who put the fun into fundraising

An interactive Internet equivalent was a natural development and a logical extension of the concept. Armed with a huge database, Trinny and Susannah had the know-how and contacts in the right places. They turned to Cable & Wireless for e-commerce expertise and acquired £600,000 in sponsorship. They developed the concept further, adding gifts, accessories and items for the home to the ever-growing portfolio, raising a further £5m in the process and currently aim to raise £20m for a cross-platform service, including interactive TV and WAP phone channels.

Pink mules for her, a red face for him

Ready2Shop is indeed a colossal business. A visit to the site is akin to having a glass of wine with a switched-on friend prior to an afternoon's shopping. Intimate without being patronising and utterly woman-to-woman. Uncompromisingly, Ready2Shop reveals all, even at the risk of a blush from a shy male surfer.

For the girl who doesn't have everything

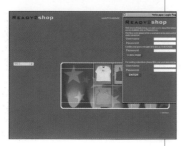

Ready2Shop builds a genuine relationship with women. Where else, for example, can you track down the current season's collections to suit someone with short legs, a large bottom and a flat chest other than at its Match to Me feature? You certainly couldn't rely on the advice from the average shop assistant with a stick insect waist and a Mel C sneer, or a well-meaning friend who secretly covets your rejects. Approachable and easy to use, Ready2Shop dispenses with the alienation that many women feel towards the Internet, whilst providing honest, tailored information and inspiration.

Human resources – your most precious asset

Trinny and Susannah attribute the success of Ready2Shop to three main factors: humanity, people/growth management and a distinctive brand. Building an appealing environment is the initial advice of Trinny and Susannah to anyone starting an Internet company – in terms of team morale as well as online look and feel. They are already reaping the benefits of hiring a first-class Human Resources expert. As Trinny says "We were expanding so fast that we desperately needed additional expertise. We were so involved in management and raising money that holding interviews for new staff became too time consuming. Having Angela on the team took a weight away from us".

Two women, one brand

Trinny and Susannah embody their brand. One is a working mother, whilst the other a manic newlywed. Which is why women find themselves at ease in sharing Trinny and Susannah's identity and beliefs.

Both are happy and willing to pass on the lessons they have learned to any would-be dot com heroes. Firstly, work out the basics. Who will look at the site? Who are they and what do they want? Acquiring additional expertise is another essential. Ready2Shop enjoys the benefit of a network of advisers, each with knowledge in the respective fields of starting a new company, marketing, technology and new media. These assets strengthen Ready2Shop's vision and provide a vital sounding board. Trinny points out to budding dot com heroes that, "Such expertise could well be closer than you think. Look amongst your contemporaries, they can be a really useful source of help, advice and inspiration".

Don't rush but don't wait either

Trinny warns, don't go to IPO too early. Whilst a private company still has the freedom to make its own choices and decisions and even make mistakes with relative impunity, that all changes after IPO. "Be ready," is Trinny's sound advice, "don't rush". By the same token, she would urge a bricks and mortar business not to ignore the Internet. "Don't fight it, use it to expand your business."

Going full circle

In Trinny's vision, the Internet in the future will be providing opportunities both on and off-line. With emphasis on Internet shopping (not least home delivery), distribution will be a massive growth sector. If FedEx's recent stock prices hike is anything to go by, she has a point. Likewise, Trinny hints that Ready2Shop need not be exclusively an Internet business. "We could use the Net to develop and then go back into traditional areas, take the concept off-line." A chain of Ready2Shop retail outlets containing a handpicked selection of the season's best, labelled by body shape and with friendly assistants in all shapes and sizes, perhaps?

But whatever happens, we can be sure that Trinny and Susannah will carry on leading from the front. They are confident that in whatever they want to expand, the technology will provide the means through either a third party or developed in-house. This gives them both roots and wings – the security of knowing they have a sound business proposition - and revenue stream – in the knowledge that whatever the future holds, Trinny and Susannah will continue to give women what they want.

Looking forward

Notwithstanding their huge success Trinny and Susannah regard their column in the *Daily Telegraph* as their greatest achievement. After all, it was their first big break.

Yet their ambition is to plan ahead rather than rest on their laurels.

Ready2Shop is indeed a colossal business. A visit to the site is akin to having a glass of wine with a switched-on friend prior to an afternoon's shopping. Intimate without being patronising and utterly woman-to-woman.

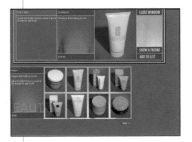

Enthusiastic, with a keen business sense and dazzling chutzpah, Benjamin Cohen, founder of the UK Jewish portal Sojewish, is one of the new generation of digerati.

The Internet market is immense; the sheer size of the opportunity often leaves even the most experienced business people bewildered over how best to tackle it. Sometimes it takes a David to conquer such a top heavy Goliath. Aged just seventeen, Benjamin Cohen is such a character. He epitomises the new digerati Netrepreneur. His site, originally called jewishnet.co.uk, is so good at reaching a targeted community that the concept is about to make him a multi-millionaire.

By simply looking around the Web, Benjamin first identified the need for a UK Jewish portal. "At the time there wasn't really a Jewish site in the UK. I think the *Jewish Chronicle* had a site but it was more of an online newspaper. There were lots of American sites but nothing British."

Humble beginnings

Benjamin started his venture with £150 borrowed from his father Richard, CEO of Epoch Software/Desktop Lawyer. The funding secured a domain name and website. "At first the site was more of a communal service, which I ran from a PC in my bedroom. My local Rabbi answered religious content questions. I then added a dating section called koshersex.co.uk."

The site's reputation grew in stature. In addition to the dating service, Benjamin added a cyber-Rabbi, yellow pages of Jewish businesses and a virtual synagogue.

A shrewd investment

Although Benjamin had the hits over the Web, he needed advice on how to develop JewishNet's commercial viability.

benjamin cohen

Community champion

sojewish.com

"One day in my father's office, I met Geoffrey Chamberlain, chairman of Epoch and Durlacher, a top investment securities group used by 365corp and Autonomy.

"I spoke to Geoffrey about JewishNet. Geoffrey rejects most of the ideas he hears. But he felt I was an exception."

"At first the site was more of a communal service, which I ran from a PC in my bedroom. My local Rabbi answered religious content questions. I then added a dating section called koshersex.co.uk."

Geoffrey told Benjamin that he was willing to set up a deal to take JewishNet further than could ever be achieved from operating out of the teenager's bedroom. "We negotiated with major Jewish newspapers in the UK as well as American sites. Michael Sinclair, a well known entrepreneur who owns the London *Jewish News*, was the keenest to help."

With support and backing from Durlacher, Epoch Software and a deal with IDesk together with the London *Jewish News*, Benjamin was ready to re-launch the site with a new name, new design and content – sojewish.com.

From heads of finance to heads of nations

News of Benjamin's idea spread far and wide. He recently met the ex-Premier of Israel – Benjamin Netenyahu.
"Mr Netenyahu heard about the site in the Israeli press. He told me that should he have been re-elected, one of his key plans was to increase Internet usage in Israel," explains Benjamin. "He thinks that there is definite potential for sojewish.com in the Israeli market as well as the US market. We are looking at taking that option forward."

After his 'A' levels, Benjamin steps into the role of CEO of cyberbritain.com, a UK specific search engine.

Benjamin's dot com heroes

"Probably Ajaz Ahmed, one of the creators of Freeserve. I think the success of JewishNet and just about every other UK start-up in the last one and half years has been spurred on by the success of Freeserve."

Benjamin is set to be a multi-millionaire before he even takes his 'A' levels. Thanks to his enthusiasm, keen business sense and sheer chutzpah, Benjamin is bound to be a model for future dot com heroes however big their ambitions.

'I think the success of JewishNet and just about every other UK start-up in the last one and half years has been spurred on by the success of Freeserve.'

This ex-Airforce
pilot exhibits all the
dedication and drive
that turns an online
venture into an online
success. He not only
spent two years
becoming an IFA but
created the AISA Direct
site, which provides
Internet-based mass
market insurance
services, himself.

james caldwell

Online insurance champion

aisa.co.uk

If you thought the world of financial services was dry and boring – think again. The highly successful independent financial services business, AISA Direct, proves that the stakes are high and potential rewards are enormous. The person behind the company is 33-year-old, ex-Airforce pilot, CEO James Caldwell.

Soon after leaving the Forces, James recognised the Internet's business potential for the UK market. "Some three years ago, whilst in the States, I undertook research on the Internet. When I returned to the UK I discovered that the financial services sector lacked real mass-market appeal. The press still view the financial services with suspicion, writing about past scandals which are mainly attributable to people who have either left the industry or are nearing retirement.

"I wanted to set things right. So I set out to qualify in financial services: it took me two years to become a fully-fledged independent financial adviser. Once qualified, drawing on my knowledge of Java script and HTML I began building an Internet site."

In touch, interactive, invaluable
James points out that future dot com heroes should feature interactive services as part of a site's integral make-up. "Interactive amenities such as calculators help customers figure out what they want online. Our extranet service is equally interactive."

AISA offers a range of financial products for a flat fee between £12.50 and £25 – all initial commission is re-invested. "Rather than trawling around for competitive quotes or the most suitable financial products, AISA saves customers time and, of course, fees," explains James.

It's well accepted that e-businesses can become overnight sensations. James cautions that this can work for, as well as increase the pressure on entrepreneurs. "We planned to launch the site at the beginning of 2000, but following press publicity which wasn't even courted, we were forced to shorten our schedule. As a result of an article in the *Sunday Times* in just three weeks we attracted in excess of £500,000 worth of investment business."

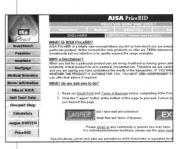

Build your team and you can build your future
James attributes his phenomenal success down to teamwork. "There is no way I could have achieved AISA's success without a great team supporting me. Teamwork for any e-business venture is imperative. This can include a virtual team of hardworking colleagues located throughout the country, incentivised through stock options and bonuses."

Only bravehearted dot com heroes need apply
James notes that e-commerce is not for the faint hearted. "To make an Internet start-up successful, you've got to invest time. It's not uncommon to work 21 days on the trot, 7am until midnight. That's really hard especially when you have a young family – as I do."

"We planned to launch the site at the beginning of 2000, but following press publicity which wasn't even courted, we were forced to shorten our schedule. As a result of an article in the *Sunday Times* in just three weeks we attracted in excess of £500,000 worth of investment business."

The new kid in town who's big in the City

Well-established financial services companies have taken note of AISA's success. Recently James was approached by a major Plc keen to invest significant capital into the company's infrastructure – enough to make AISA a household name overnight. "Providing we receive a cash injection, by the end of 2000 we plan to employ around 45 people," promises James.

A name to remember – a future to bank upon

James advises any business planning a Web-wide presence to aim to build a powerful, memorable brand. His strategy seems to be working. "People question why the company is called 'AISA' Direct – it's spelt differently on purpose. Customers think about the spelling and remember the name."

James would dearly like to link the insurance supply chain online. "We've got high-level contacts with all the major insurance companies. We're just waiting for the government to approve digital signatures – and for the insurance companies to get fully online."

"My overriding vision for AISA's future is to be the largest financial services site. As an independent financial services company we have the major advantage that we sell everything from everyone and have access to all the insurance companies. Our business plan is clearly set for growth."

Self-confessed 'traditional rebel', Charles Fallon is the strategic brain and Co-founder of Pets Pyjamas, the site that's catnip to pet owners. A charming blend of adventure and practicality, Charles is the customer's champion in the pet world.

charles fallon

Pet portal pioneer

petspyjamas.com

If there's one thing that makes Charles Fallon, Co-founder of petspyjamas.com laugh, it's hearing other companies complain about how the Internet upsets their traditional business model. "Of course it does!" he replies, "You'll just have to create a new one!"

This willingness to innovate is just one of the things that makes Pets Pyjamas such a worthwhile site for pet owners and animal lovers alike. Packed with customer-focused propositions, including half price pet insurance and next day delivery, and offering an incredible choice at unbeatable prices, Pets Pyjamas is to pet products what Viking Direct is to stationery.

It all began in 1997 when Charles met Alastair Angus, who owned a number of businesses in the stationery business and had seen how Viking Direct had transformed it through direct selling. Charles, meanwhile, had earned a reputation as an innovator, having spent ten years at Saatchi and Saatchi Advertising, and in 1995 founded Saatchi and Saatchi Vision, where he first became involved with e-commerce. By 1997 he was ready for a venture of his own.

The timing was perfect. Alastair wanted to sell pet products direct. He teamed up with Charles who added strategic expertise to Alastair's negotiation skills and financial flair. By 1998, Pets Pyjamas was launched online as well as in a catalogue form.

The service got off to the best possible start. Their idea had already won the *Sunday Times* 3i Catapult Business Competition, earning the partnership their first round of equity investment. This was supplemented by Chase Capital Partners who syndicated the investment and, by doing so, brought a wide range of experience and skills to maximise the chances of success.

Enthusiasm that leaps off the page

Today, the site still reflects the founders' enthusiasm flowing in waves from the pages. Yet despite its visual and emotional appeal to anyone who has ever owned so much as a goldfish, Charles remains pragmatic about what makes the service such a success. "Fulfilment is the key. Creating a sense of community is all very well," he asserts, "but delivery comes first."

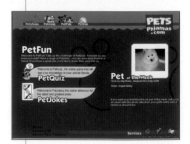

Constantly bombarded with requests for help from wannabes, Charles would recommend a combination of adventurous practicality. "Firstly, don't just copy an idea, innovate. Secondly, get the right mix of people. Thirdly, be careful in the choice of backers. Most importantly, create an innovative customer proposition."

One vision. Multiple channels.

As with Viking Direct, Pets Pyjamas currently offers a choice of paper-based catalogue and Web channels. Soon this will be supplemented by Pets Pyjamas via interactive TV. In fact, Charles envisages the day when television, not necessarily the PC, will be the main communications interface – especially with the advent of broadband. And, as with television, the public will become less concerned with the communications technology itself and more with the content. "We don't think 'I'm going to receive signals from the TV network', we think 'What shall I watch tonight?'"

Deliver the goods, not just the experience

Returning to his concerns about fulfilment, Charles believes logistical rather than technological concerns, will be the biggest challenge of all. As he points out, "Consumers are buying products, not an 'Internet shopping experience' and expect fast, efficient delivery. Perhaps we will return to the days when groceries were delivered on separate days. Fish on Friday. Meat on Saturday. And dog collars on Sundays?"

A new lease of life for brands

He also predicts that the role of marketing and brands will become more important than ever – a rebuttal of the fear that the Internet spells the death of brands. In fact, he's convinced that the opposite is true. "The brand will become the only differentiator," he asserts, and he should know. Pet food for example, is sold almost wholly on brand values rather than the actual formula of the product.

Yet despite his practical concerns about the fulfilment side of e-commerce, Charles remains an entrepreneur, ready to experiment and take risks. He's well aware that the scene will become more 'establishment' and conformist as it settles down, but for now at least, the opportunities are there for 'traditional rebels' like himself to innovate. "It's so refreshing when I meet someone who really thinks creatively."

No wonder his personal dot com hero is Nicholas Negroponte, one of the founders of the cutting-edge *Wired* magazine. His book 'Being Digital. The roadmap for survival on the Information Superhighway' changed the way Charles saw the future – and the direction of his career.

Identifying with the underdog

While Charles admits to a healthy dose of paranoia which keeps him on his toes and ensures that new ideas keep coming, he still has the sense of humour that makes Pets Pyjamas so charming. Among his anecdotes is the one about the woman who ordered coats for her dogs, seven blue and one grey. Just a few days after delivery she emailed back to say that the dogs in blue coats were picking on the one in grey...

Although he's modest about his successes, Charles is also disarmingly honest about his failures. "We've made huge numbers of mistakes, been too slow, too fast, so trusting we've been taken to the cleaners."

Not many Netrepreneurs of his stature would make that admission, but to Charles Fallon, it's all part of the learning experience.

"Fulfilment is the key. Creating a sense of community is all very well," he asserts, "but delivery comes first. Or at least within three working days."

First Tuesday, Co-founded by John Browning, is a global network created by new media entrepreneurs for new media entrepreneurs. It is a resource which helps entrepreneurs grow their companies faster and more effectively.

When did you first get involved in the Net?

I started writing about the Internet for *The Economist* in the late 1980s. My first Internet email account was with the Well in 1990. I got excited by the Web when it was still text-based, and point-and-click involved typing in numbers. I wrote the first article on the Web for *Wired* when Marc Andreesen released Mosaic for Windows and Mac – and received a flame from Marc that the screen shot should have been better.

First Tuesday evolved out of a cocktail party organised by Adam Gold, Nick Denton, Mark Davies and Julie Meyer in October of 1998. I got formally involved when Mark Davies left for a year's travelling in December of 1999.

Key behind site

Timing, honesty, human connections.

How is it unique?

First Tuesday is the only global network created by new media entrepreneurs for new media entrepreneurs.

What are your three top tips for building an Internet business?

1. Find out how to use the technology to do something better than it's been done before. (This shouldn't be hard, given revolutionary and fast-moving technology.)
2. Figure out who benefits most from your innovation and what value you are creating for them.
3. Build your innovation and communicate its virtues to those who benefit. Remember that timing is all.

john browning

The Connected Netrepreneur

firsttuesday.com

We organise events over five continents and provide services to help Internet entrepreneurs to grow their companies more quickly – including raising money, hiring talent and finding offices – via our Web site, firsttuesday.com.

What is your greatest achievement?

I like to believe that the greatest is still to come.

If you're too early, the technology is too clunky and people won't get it. If you're too late, you'll more than likely be fighting a competitor with a lead. Because everything takes time to build, getting the timing right means always managing as if you're living six months in the future.

How did you secure finances?

By asking for them.

Any advice for other start-ups?

Always hire people smarter and better than you are.

Advice for a traditional business

Understand what the Internet can do for your customers and build that into your product or service.

Your vision of the Web's future

The Internet is disappearing in the way that all successful technologies disappear. It is becoming ubiquitous and as taken for granted as air, gravity, telephone or television. Not just everyone will be connected to everyone else, but everything will be connected to everything else. So instead of communicating to get things done – for example picking up the phone to track a package – we'll do things that communicate. The package will tell the world (via the Web) where it is at any given moment.

Golden opportunities

Most people now work in white-collar, information-processing jobs and the Internet is revolutionising the ways in which information is processed. Opportunities abound: creating more efficient supply chains for businesses; embedding information into physical products to educate and delight customers; creating a stronger sense of human community and connection.

How will you stay ahead?

As best I can.

Any Net predictions?

Digital bandwidth is becoming a commodity and, like all commodities, will come under increasing price pressure as the world's networks compete to carry bits. This transforms the economics of media. Not just by making them cheaper but also by making it easy to create the whole infrastructure, from production studios to the equipment to carry the signals zipping across the wires. Old media had to build all that for themselves. New media, from smart phones to MP3 players and beyond can take transmission capacity from the Net. This is unleashing a vast wave of innovation aimed at getting us just the right information in just the right form to be most useful.

Personal hero

Ken Thompson, Dennis Ritchie, Brian Kernighan and Doug McIlroy and the others at AT&T Bell Labs who invented the UNIX operating system. They made it all possible.

Favourite sites

FT.com and wsj.com – for news

faqs.org – the Web helps itself help you

elibrary.com – online clippings and information

sltrib.com – for old time's sake (I'm from Utah)

ntk.net – intelligent Internet news written by former stand-up comics and of course, firsttuesday.com

Greatest thing about the Net

It enables you to be in constant touch with the world and its information.

Worst thing

It enables you to be in constant touch with the world and its information.

What inspires you?

The future.

What should inspire others?

Their dreams.

Other interests

My family, skiing, riding, computer science and artificial intelligence, business history, sleep.

"Not just everyone will be connected to everyone else, but everything will be connected to everything else."

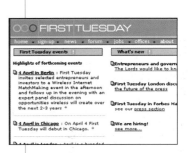

Providing a complete Web-based wedding service, Confetti is a gift to engaged couples. Its brief, according to 'consumer-obsessed' Co-founder David Lethbridge, is to provide a value-added service that simply wouldn't be available elsewhere.

david lethbridge

Special e-occasions

confetti.co.uk

For most couples, planning their wedding provides the blessed opportunity to realise many dreams. It sets them on an uncharted course that calls for joint manoeuvring to arrive safely at the nuptial destination. Yet, how many are so determined to make it through the maiden voyage? Some wedding preparations take months or years to organise. "Most couples eventually come to the conclusion that there must be a simpler way. Thanks to Confetti, there is."

A big idea for the big day

David Lethbridge and Andrew Doe, Co-founders of Confetti, offer consumers a value-added online wedding service that helps them save time and money. Describing himself as 'consumer obsessed', David is utterly on the customer's side. If you're a harassed bride, with a wedding to plan, a budget to maximise and high expectations to meet, turning to Confetti is not only a huge relief, it's a blessing.

Offering a concerted combination of content, commerce and community, Confetti gives instant access to support and information. It provides the means for couples to share pre-wedding planning, hair-tearing experiences, search from a vast database of suppliers, collect quotes and make arrangements, quickly and conveniently. It's the very model of a successful, consumer-focused Internet service, which not only offers value to customers and suppliers alike but simply could not be available in any other form.

Obsessed by consumers, driven by customers

Exploiting his 'consumer obsession', it comes as no surprise that David urges both start-ups and traditional businesses to adopt the same ethic. For start-ups, he advises them to develop not just a good idea, but one that delivers real benefit to the user. He also recommends that finances are not just to provide a sound technology infrastructure – but more to deliver on promises.

Invest in value, not just technology

Having recently gained $12m of Venture Capital in his second round of funding, Andrew provides a piece of advice for other Net entrepreneurs. "Ensure your backers can add value by giving you expertise and support."

For traditional businesses, his expert advice is: "Don't treat your website as a token gesture". He finds that many other organisations just hand their Web projects over to the IT department and expect them to get on with it. To Andrew and David, passion is an essential ingredient to bring a website to life.

"Ensure your backers can add value by giving you expertise and support."

Let consumers show you the way

David's predictions about the Internet and his own plans for the future are, as you might expect, based around offering people what they want. Opportunities are to be found by "following demographics online". New groups of consumers will come to the Web and the key to satisfying them is to offer content, community and commerce; a combination that has established Confetti in the limelight.

Last but not least, David makes some interesting observations about the sense of community that exists among Internet businesses. While he agrees that in time the environment will probably become more competitive and cut-throat, there is currently a culture of supportiveness. People are prepared to help each other, to provide council, and inspiration.

In essence, this is what he offers with Confetti. No wonder he loves it.

Andrew Doe – Co-founder

With her business partner, Ernst Malmsten, Kajsa Leander launched in 1997 the Internet bookstore bokus.com in Sweden. Her next 'creation' was boo.com, an entirely new e-business concept offering sports and streetwear on the Net. boo.com is currently one of the first pan-European Net companies with a presence in North America.

kajsa leander

E-fashion diva

boo.com

'Second generation' e-business entrepreneurs are rare. Most are fully engaged in running their Net business. Yet Kajsa Leander belongs to that rare group. With her business partner Ernst Malmsten, Kajsa launched in 1997 the Internet bookstore bokus.com in Sweden. It was directed at students who were already computer and Internet savvy, and in need of textbooks. The business steadily grew and within a very short time secured some 100,000 customers – a resounding success.

Soon competitors such as amazon.com moved in. By 1998, a strategic decision was taken and bokus.com was sold for a handsome return.

A surprising creation

Kajsa's primary ambition is 'to create'. Her next 'creation' was boo.com, an entirely new e-business concept offering sports and streetwear on the Net. boo.com is currently one of the first pan-European Net companies with a presence in North America. Via the Net it offers a distinctive range of goods to 19 countries, involving seven different languages.

The key to launching boo.com was enrolling heavyweight suppliers whose brands were still sensitive to the relatively new Internet channel. "Once they knew more about the whole concept, they readily agreed to go ahead," says Kajsa.

The brilliantly designed site provides a broad range of products including premium brands such as Puma, DKNY Active, Moschino, New Balance, and Maharishi. Aimed at 'techno savvy', fast lane living 18 to 35 year olds, boo.com is the modern response to page-based, fashion catalogue shopping and traditional youth brand retailing.

Growing bigger and better by the day

With the excellent track record achieved with bokus.com Kajsa and Ernst faced no problem in procuring financial backing for boo.com, which was provided by JP Morgan.

boo.com is spreading to new markets including Italy, Spain, and Latin America. Kajsa explains: "We've built a great platform and created a strong brand. Next we want to get even better at what we're doing." Kajsa adds, "High bandwidth will make a tremendous difference in terms of attracting new users and encouraging people to shop more on the Internet. This, together with digital TV and increased use of WAP (Wireless Application Protocol) phones will make e-commerce even easier, offering a wider appeal and therefore increased popularity."

The good, the bad and the passionate

In Kajsa's view the best aspect of the Internet is the access it confers to products and information. And the worst? "Being in its infancy, it's quite slow and can be very frustrating." Good and practical ideas as well as open-minded people inspire Kajsa. She is also keen to take on challenges – not least from people who question her. She considers it essential to have a passion for what you do and at the same time enjoy it.

"We've built a great platform and created a strong brand. Next we want to get even better at what we're doing." Kajsa adds, "High bandwidth will make a tremendous difference in terms of attracting new users and encouraging people to shop more on the Internet. This, together with digital TV and increased use of WAP (Wireless Application Protocol) phones will make e-commerce even easier, offering a wider appeal and therefore increased popularity."

Fashionable tips

Her key to successful management? "Never be afraid to recruit people who are better qualified than you. It's essential to get expertise from different areas, from people with experience that contrasts with your own. I think I'm a nice boss. I have fun with my staff but I can be demanding, and expect very high-quality output from my employees."

To those setting up a new Internet business Kajsa's top tips are "to write a solid business plan, continue to challenge it; make sure it works before you go any further; and to get some money behind the project. Above all, believe in it and do it!"

In the case of traditional businesses attracted to get into the Internet, the major issues to combat, as advocated by Kajsa, are the smooth transfer of the brand to the Internet, and targeting a completely different group of consumers.

Naturally cultivated heroes

Kajsa's personal dot com hero is Tina Brown, founder of *Talk* magazine, for taking the risk of leaving the UK to set up her own business in the USA. Her favourite websites are the *New York Times* site for news and business information and Amazon for books and CDs online.

Outside of work and the Internet, Kajsa's hobby is gardening – certainly an unusual past-time for someone so engrossed in a fast paced business world. But she explains "I enjoy gardening because it is so different from my everyday work life. It's slow – you can't hurry nature – and is the complete opposite of working at boo. It's great to enjoy a change of pace at the weekends."

For Tim Jackson,
founder of the QXL online
auction site, customer
satisfaction is not enough.
Customer enjoyment is
what he's after, providing
a service that people
really want.

tim jackson

E-auctioneer

qxl.com

When did you first get involved in the Net?
As a journalist writing about it for the *Independent* in 1994 and the *Financial Times* in 1995.

What is your greatest achievement?
Recruiting a great team of people at qxl.com.

Key behind site
Providing a service that people really want, the ability to buy and sell things, on the Internet.

How is it unique?
Wow, loads of things. We've got a huge community of buyers and sellers. We price varyingly according to supply and demand – in a way that just couldn't be done without offer value-added features like escrow and security and ratings that help people do business. And we've got a whole range of products and services that make the process fun. Auctions are the only kind of online shopping I've ever come across that people actually enjoy!

What are your three top tips for building an Internet business?
Don't start it with your own money – I did that, and it's incredibly stressful. Hire great people and be willing to give them a substantial stake in the company. Give up any chance of seeing your friends or family while you build the business.

How did you secure finances?
Nobody except me would back it at first. Six months later, from private individuals.

Any advice for other start-ups?
Pick an investor you really trust who you believe can help grow the business.

Advice for a traditional business
Watch out – the Internet poses threats as well as opportunities.

Your vision of the Web's future
Always-on real-time access for everyone, wherever they are.

Golden opportunities
Wow – too many to name.

How will you stay ahead?
By executing better than anyone else – doing a great job and really caring about the customer.

Personal hero
Jeff Bezos – he's obsessed with customer satisfaction.

Favourite sites
amazon.com, sec.gov, qxl.com

Greatest thing about the Net
It's changing the world.

Worst thing
It's not always changing it for the better. We need to cherish pre-Internet things like letters on paper, meeting people face to face, and taking walks in the park.

What inspires you?
Music. Scenery. Kids.

What should inspire others?
Non-technology things. People. Second-hand books. Architecture.

Soundbite
I'm an analyst, not a nerd. But I also like to get things done.

Any quirks or interesting facts?
I once posed with a cabbage in *Harpers & Queen* magazine.

Other interests
I've got little kids – with work and sleep, there's little time for anything else.

Expansive and easy-going, Alexander Broich, head of BOL UK, is enchanted by the Internet's possibilities but remains pragmatic about how quickly consumers will allow it to happen. Alexander is a man who asks "why not?" rather than "why?"

alexander broich

Multi-media adventurer

bol.com

Alexander Broich, the UK Managing Director of bol.com, the online book and music store, is passionate about books, music and above all, e-commerce. He was first introduced to the Internet in 1994 by his girlfriend. "The technology was slow, it wasn't very visually arresting but with faster technology I recognised it had terrific commercial possibilities."

At the time, Alexander worked for a consulting company. To him the Internet was still a private, rather than career interest. Despite being offered excellent jobs with BMW and Lufthansa, his passion for the Web led him to a meeting with Thomas Middelhoff, CEO of the New Media division of Bertelsmann, owners of Random House and BMG. With a shared vision to elevate Bertelsmann into a multimedia company, Alexander was duly appointed Head of Corporate Development for New Media. He spent the next two years initiating new media projects, including partnerships with AOL and Lycos. Soon Alexander's stature in the burgeoning Internet industry reached the point where, by the age of just 30, he founded Health On Line, a Net-based subscription service for doctors.

Today, Alexander is Managing Director of BOL UK, one of the Internet's favourite book and music stores. It is his third company built from scratch and a wholly owned division of Bertelsmann. BOL's success relies on more than just technology. "It is a shopping experience rather than an order service. Whilst it offers discounts, choice and fast delivery, it also combines technological fulfilment with a welcoming atmosphere and user-friendly environment. Customers need no technical expertise other than to point and click – a vital advantage when selling such a universal product to millions of people."

First a pioneer – always an adventurer

Expansive, easy-going and keen to evangelise the opportunities of the Internet, Alexander offers three pieces of advice for anyone building an online business:

- Be responsive and react quickly
- Be patient; deals can be closed quickly but the results can take longer
- And be prepared to find the answers for yourself by taking risks and learning from mistakes

Some are afraid of uncertainty, many hate taking risks, but to a pioneering spirit like Alexander, it's an adventure. "There's no blueprint for an Internet business. After all, what could be more exciting than a business in which saying 'I don't know, let's try it' is the name of the game?"

The right balance of people and technology

As a businessman rather than a technological guru, Alexander is pragmatic about what he calls the 'inherent inertia in human nature'. Whilst he advises start-up companies to never under-estimate the speed of technology, he also recommends not to over-estimate the speed of people. In his experience, the former, always moves quicker than the latter. "A site may be fast and functional, with a host of innovations and a unique proposition, but people must be prepared – and know about it. Good ideas take seconds, but building a strong and successful business – what an online company is all about – takes time."

"There's no blueprint for an Internet business. After all, what could be more exciting than a business in which saying 'I don't know, let's try it' is the name of the game?"

The new revolution

As for the future of the Web, Alexander envisages a world in which everything and everyone is connected. "Forget current e-commerce disciplines, soon there will be revolutionary methods for interaction, communication and transaction. The PC will become just one of dozens of devices that interface with the Web. Mobility, wires and speed will no longer be the limiting factors which they are today". Alexander's specific predictions for BOL are kept open. At any given time he has several potential future scenarios and attendant strategies ready to deploy when the state of play dictates.

A lateral choice of hero

Alexander's choice of personal dot com hero echoes his broadminded approach towards the future. Rather than a person, he casts his vote in favour of a genre: the early adopter. "They try something because it's new. They don't ask 'why' or worry about the technology. Early adopters drive development; they have vision."

Alexander believes that rather than simply a channel for traditional media, a website is a medium in its own right, with its own rules and standards. Which is why he admires the CNN site. He likes the way it is designed specifically for the Web, how it is always up to date and makes innovative use of multimedia such as video.

CNN's site mirrors Alexander's vision for the Internet as a means to connect people, rather than convey transactions. For example, he knows that without email he would have certainly lost touch with an old friend. Yet, by the same token, the ubiquitous message 'website found, waiting for reply' suggests that in terms of speed, there is still a long way to go. However, Alexander is optimistic about the current state of technology "The Internet is as slow today as cars were in 1905. But look at them now".

The consummate achiever

The chance to actively participate in the shaping process is, in Alexander's own words, "what gets me up for work so early". For him, the opportunity to 'do it' rather than simply read about it, is the ultimate adventure. Clearly, when eventually someone writes his life story to be sold via BOL, one of the enduring characteristics that will emerge from his remarkable tale will be that Alexander consistently recognises real potential rather than commercial hype.

Thanks to his passion for the Web and tenacity in business, he will remain an enduring dot com hero who achieves goals rather than simply promises todeliver ideals.

365 Corporation provides content and communication services for the sport, entertainment and lifestyle sectors – or 'passion centres'. Founder Dan Thompson is convinced that quality content, created specifically for the medium, is the key to an online business.

dan thompson

All day, every day

365corp.com

The workaholic with a passion for commitment

The 365 Corporation home site describes the focus for its content and communication services as 'passion centres' within the areas of sports, entertainment and lifestyle. It's a description that could equally apply to Dan Thompson himself, 365's founder and resident visionary. Utterly passionate about his subject, dedicated to his customers, the word 'committed' seems almost too casual a term.

A service for passionate people

That's because Dan is one of those rare people in the Internet industry with a crystal-clear vision of what he wants to achieve and, therefore, what 365 is all about. The answer is quality content and a visit to one of the sites, such as football365, is ample proof of Dan's single-minded dedication to giving people what they want. The site is passionate about football, it provides information and services of a depth and editorial quality unsurpassed on the Internet, it's interactive, up-to-date, accessible and welcoming. What's more, it has obviously been designed for the medium of the Internet itself which make it work uniquely well in its context.

Swept away by the digital movement

This preoccupation with content was actually the reason for Dan's first involvement with the Internet. Working first in the music industry, then in video and computer games, Dan could see how the digitisation of content could transform the whole concept of entertainment. He also spotted the potential of the Internet, not just as a medium for a new breed of content but as an interactive channel that could reach out to a vast global audience, at very little cost.

From nightmare to millions

Never a man to sit and dream, Dan promptly gave up his job and founded 365 with a select team of like-minded colleagues, who were, as he describes "all going in the same direction". But, with very little money and huge pressures to prove their business model, surviving the first year was, despite being a "complete nightmare" a tremendous achievement. The early days weren't helped by the fact that outside investors were nowhere to be found and the team were forced to dig into their own pockets. Only Durlachers were interested and they were followed in the second year by more investors, but no Venture Capitalists, who still weren't interested. They're probably sorry now though, because 365 raised £60m at IPO in December 1999.

Tangible service in the intangible medium of cyberspace

This success has validated Dan's conviction that the key to an online business is the ability to create quality content and take it over multiple channels. His vision of the Internet of the future is of a vast "network of content, services, interactivity and communications, accessed seamlessly through multiple access points". Always there, it will form the backdrop to our lives. As he points out, the Internet gets rid of intermediaries and so the businesses who can "create and own a destination point", providing a service that people actually want, will be the winners. Dan's 'passion centres' are the embodiment of this conviction.

Business comes first

But Dan means business, and passion alone won't pay the rent. Acknowledging the vital contribution his own team makes and calling them his personal dot com heroes, he'd recommend a new Internet company first equips itself with a top management team and second, has a genuinely profitable business model with a proper margin. While the Internet makes communication and international marketing easier and more affordable than ever, without the traditional cost and distribution barriers of terrestrial business, you still need to make money.

In fact, in today's increasingly competitive market, with ever-more savvy consumers with high expectations of content, service and delivery, he'd recommend funding, as a necessity rather than a luxury.

The man with better things to do...

But whilst Dan enjoys so much about the Internet and its potential for transforming our lives, he's less keen on the constant speculation about its future considering it time consuming and unnecessary. Famous as a workaholic and "for driving himself and other people too hard", Dan is obviously chomping at the bit to get back to work.

The 365 Corporation home site describes the focus for its content and communication services as 'passion centres' within the areas of sports, entertainment and lifestyle.

Businesses who can "create and own a destination point", providing a service that people actually want, will be the winners.

jungle.com's CEO and founder, Steve Bennett, sees himself as a customer service, rather than dot com, hero. jungle.com offers everything from CDs to DVDs, free email and Net access, free delivery and a loyalty bonus scheme.

steve bennett

It's a jungle out there

jungle.com

Steve Bennett, CEO of jungle.com would like to be remembered as a customer service hero rather than a dot com hero. He explains, "The choice I aim at providing is an enhanced shopping service, rather than Internet experience."

Whilst Steve is passionate about the Internet, he is also enchanted by its possibilities as another channel to market and so providing yet an additional choice to his customers. Steve's track record bears this out. His other company, Software Warehouse was the first of its kind to sell over the Internet, creating its own online catalogue system in the process. Initially the site attracted around three online orders a day. Currently Software Warehouse takes over 3,000 daily and has an annual turnover of over £100m.

It's a jungle out there

Steve's latest venture, jungle.com, offers a vast range of titles, from CDs to DVDs as well as free email, delivery and Internet access plus a loyalty bonus scheme. The site's Product Advisory Wizard (PAW) technology provides independent guidance and support. Steve explains "At last, customers can comfortably find what they want without feeling intimidated as often happens in a typical high-street megastore".

A memorable brand, a consistent message

Besides its online wizardry and memorable URL, jungle.com's success owes much to its '3D brand' and consistent marketing. Steve explains, "Our logo features a distinctive paw print and eye-catching green colour. Equally unforgettable is our signature tune: The lion sleeps tonight".

Steve advises anyone starting an online venture to aim for consistency in every aspect of business. His other tip is to make good use of available experience. In his case, that adds up to over a decade's worth of personal business experience, supported by a highly competent management team.

Ideas and expertise – the ideal combination

Steve concedes that the Internet's future lies with the big corporate companies. "Whilst someone with an original idea can be trading online within just a few days, it's the big companies, with their customer management skills and wealth of business resources which will ultimately dominate the scene."

Steve acknowledges that a successful Internet enterprise demands more than limited resources of a person on his own. In his role as jungle.com's visionary leader, he devotes several hours daily in learning and exploring new technologies and ideas, so staying ahead of the increasingly competitive game. He delegates the routine running of jungle.com to the management team, while he develops ideas to challenge the competition.

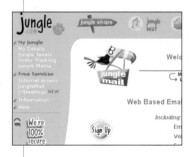

Get into the Internet, even if you don't get onto it

Steve urges all business, even those whose products and services are unlikely to be sold online, to try to understand Internet technology and the implications that the World Wide Web extends to the commercial world. "Whilst people are happy to buy music titles from a website, they are unlikely to buy jewellery. But having a entrepreneur on the board could open up all sorts of possibilities." Steve predicts that "within five years, everyone will be on the Internet, whether they know it or not. It's vital that businesses come to terms with it now."

And that's straight from the lion who rules the jungle...

ThinkNatural, the company that brings us natural healthcare products and information at a click, is the creation of Carol Dukes, Co-founder and CEO of this popular site.

carol dukes

Natural entrepreneur
thinknatural.com

When did you first get involved in the Net?

In 1993 I joined the media company EMAP plc. I decided to focus on looking at the opportunities presented by electronic media – then mainly fixed media such as CD-ROMs. We ran a few trial services on the early online services such as Compuserve and Delphi, and I was in the offices of Delphi when one of their people came in with great excitement and proceeded to show us all the very first Mosaic Web browser.

I went straight back to EMAP and told them that we had to start working on developing some services for the Internet platform, which until then had not been a consumer proposition at all. Within months they had backed me to set up one of the first ever Internet publishing teams, which went on to become EMAP Online.

What is your greatest achievement?

With my colleague Emma Crowe, we established ThinkNatural.com in four months from a standing start. This involved in no particular order: hiring from scratch a team of 20 plus people; finding, negotiating and kitting out a warehouse and office property; outsourcing and managing the delivery of a complete e-commerce system with a dynamically published website, payment clearance, integrated accounts and inventory management; dealing with all the legal structuring of the company; buying hardware; negotiating hosting, bandwidth; planning strategy, creative branding, product development and marketing; organising delivery arrangements and packaging; getting computers, phones and desks; structuring the accounts; doing market research; putting in place supply arrangements with over 40 suppliers, getting 5,000 product lines in stock, organising a team of people to data entry every word written on the product packaging, and take and process digital images of each product; managing investor relations; licensing three encyclopedias from Dorling Kindersley and data re-engineering their contents into a database-friendly format; finding and recruiting and commissioning a team of editorial staff, journalists, practictioners to write for the site; negotiating distribution deals with all the major (and minor) portals, PR activity in business, trade and consumer press, all the data protection, health and safety stuff, trying to develop a company culture and take care of our staff. And ordering the stationery.

I am also very proud of the teams I built, and their achievements, at Carlton Online and Emap Online.

The key behind our business is (a) using the Web to offer a much wider range of (natural healthcare) products, which are often hard to find, than is possible through a traditional shop and (b) providing searchable, browsable information alongside the products.

What are your three top tips for building an Internet business?

1. If you can't do it fast, don't do it at all.
2. Respect the technology and your technologists. If you refer to technologists as 'anoraks' then you're not in the right mindset.
3. Have a clear proposition for the customer and focus on that relentlessly.

"Everyone should dance to their own tune – it's just a case of hearing it through the clutter of things like money, convention, fear and corporate rules."

Any advice for start-ups?

Be clear about what you're trying to achieve, think it through from the customer's point of view, think it through in terms of what it requires in the supply chain and get a good finance director on board.

Advice for traditional businesses

You have three options:

1 Set up a completely independent operation, and then leave it entirely alone so that it can move quickly and flexibly, or

2 Invest in strategic stakes in independent start-ups, or

3 Sit back, amass cash and then buy up the winners when the dust has settled.

What is your vision of the Web's future?

I believe that digital businesses will have to provide services which the customer will access through a range of devices including DAB radio, WAP phones, the Web over PC, the Web over TV, fridge etc, interactive TV platforms etc etc. The challenge will be to make the service operational and user-friendly over all these types of access points and to accept that the customer will be the one in control of how they experience your service.

Golden opportunities

Getting the final link in home delivery right.

How will you stay ahead?

Good old fashioned virtues of listening to customers to ensure that we expand the range in the right way, that we continually improve and refine our information, and providing great customer service.

Net predictions

Current perceptions of B2B versus B2C will be replaced by a more thoughtful analysis of sectors which are good for e-commerce and sectors which are bad for e-commerce. The market leaders in the 'good' sectors will be the new blue chips.

Personal dot com heroes

Lots! David Arculus who backed me when he was MD of EMAP even though he didn't understand what I was going on about, and who years later backed me in setting up ThinkNatural when he did understand what I was going on about!

Roger Green who was one of the very first people to see the importance of the Internet and who has kept the faith at Emap ever since.

All those inspiring people who used to go to the parties in Cyberia and who made the Internet space such a fun and compelling place to work: Charles Ashley, Eva Pascoe, David Rowe, Ivan Pope, Steve Bowbrick, Keith Teare, Eamonn Wilmott, Jackie Bissel, Marion Buckley – the list goes on. They know who they are!

Greatest thing about the Net

There is still a sense of co-operation both in the industry and amongst Web users. It's fantastic that this is still a very strong seam throughout the Web environment. Some newcomers don't understand this and I really hope that they don't destroy this wonderful place where the values of sharing, mutual helpfulness and working together are pre-eminent. This is what built the Web.

Worst thing

Operations where the front end isn't backed up by the back end. Web businesses have to understand that they are still businesses, albeit with exciting new channels to market.

What inspires you?

New things – I don't like doing the same thing over and over again. And people – I like people.

What should inspire others?

Everyone should dance to their own tune – it's just a case of hearing it through the clutter of things like money, convention, fear and corporate rules.

Soundbite

I'm not a perfectionist. If it's good enough, then let's keep moving on.

Quirks, stories etc?

A random selection - for this you have to understand that I have absolutely no sense of direction whatsoever. So a few snapshots: trading punches with muggers in the backstreets of Fez (I was lost), driving across the manicured lawns of Cliveden in the middle of the night (I was lost), leaping onto the back of the motorbike of a stranger in the backstreets of Harare then realising that I had no money and didn't know the address of my hotel (I was lost), pushing a loaded luggage trolley at speed across a number of six lane highways at Los Angeles airport (I was lost), telling a Ukrainian that I'd been 3 days in Moscow and not yet had any vodka (I was soon lost)...

Interests other than the Net

Food and wine, gardening, conservation and conversation.

Despite his reputation as a Web guru, Upmystreet's Chairman Ian Stewart lives in the real world. Providing useful information about local areas, from restaurants to schools, Upmystreet helps customers get more from their lives, via the Internet.

ian charles stewart

Area viewer

upmystreet.com

When did you first get involved in the Net?

Introduced by friends to email in 1987, then Venture Capitalist and as fund manager of the Pearson new media fund 1988–1992.

What is your greatest achievement?

Maintaining a happy and healthy family life whilst helping to found and build: *Wired* magazine, upmystreet.com, The Digital Village, Sunbather, Empty Space et al.

Key behind site

Upmystreet.com is trying to provide you with everything you need to know about where you live and how best to live your life there.

How is it unique?

Mediated, objective, community-based, database-supported guidance on where you live, where you should eat, what local mini-cab services to use, what local schools are best for your children, where best to buy products and services near where you are, now.

What are your three top tips for building an Internet business?

Put together a great management team that can genuinely do all the things you will need to do and raise more capital than you think you need. Start by doing one thing really, really well and only then try doing other things.

How did you secure finances?

Ourselves, then friends and family, then VCs and corporate investors and strategic partners.

Any advice for other start-ups?

Focus on the quality of everything you do; the rest will follow (but keep an eye on how good is good enough...).

Advice for a traditional business

Accept the need for change or prepare now your exit strategy. If you accept the need for real change, then go and find people who understand how to make this change, to help you.

Your vision of the Web's future

As ubiquitous as running water and electricity, and as fundamental. Many things will be easier. Certain things (e.g. getting away from it all, or autocratic tyrannical government) may be harder. As we eliminate ever more of the tedium in our lives, there will be more soul searching, and perhaps more time, therefore, to indulge in angst!

Golden opportunities

Greater access to personalised learning.

How will you stay ahead?

Try always to listen and learn.

Any Net predictions?

That most of the dot com companies of today will not exist in ten years' time. That most of the top fifty companies of the year 2050 do not yet exist today. That we ain't seen nothin' yet.

Favourite sites

Anything that actually delivers on promises; Amazon, CNN, Hotbot. Sites that do things that are not possible without the Net e.g. accompany.com, eBay, upmystreet.com.

Greatest thing about the Net

The access it gives anyone to everything.

Worst thing

The access it gives everyone to saying anything.

What inspires you?

Great risk-taking entrepreneurs who are able to take an idea, break new ground, and turn it all into a business.

What should inspire others?

The successes of 'other others'!

James Slavet, Co-founder
and CEO of guru.com
envisages changing the
way the world works
with guru.com, the site
for connecting
independent professionals
to each other.

james slavet

Professional e-matchmaker

When did you first get involved in the Net?

I first got involved with the Net through my work at Vivid Studios, a Web development shop, starting in 1993. Vivid's offices were and still are right off South Park in San Francisco, in the same building as Wired magazine, in the heart of what came to be known at Multimedia Gulch. At the time, we were mostly developing CD-ROM projects for clients, by 1994/1995, Vivid's project work starting morphing from CD-ROMs to Internet-based project work.

What is your greatest achievement?

Playing a role in taking guru.com from an idea hatched out of the living room (back when my bedroom was the conference room!) with no customers, no team, no product... to a very real and vibrant business that is making an impact on peoples' lives. Helping to attract a terrific group of employees, investors and board members to get our business off to the right start. Seeing the excitement and commitment today of other folks working at guru.com who continue to grow the business and build on the initial vision for the company. Walking through the halls of guru.com headquarters today and hearing other members of the team give 'the pitch' of what our business is all about to potential partners and customers. Realising how far we've come – and believing that we're just at chapter two or so of a long, exciting story.

Key behind site

At guru.com, we want to help change the way the world works. guru.com is the leading online marketplace connecting expert freelancers and consultants (from virtual CEOs to graphic designers, and everything in between) with contract projects. We also help these independent professionals, 'gurus', run their businesses, through providing them with back office tools (like a time & expense application), deals on products and services (like insurance) and expert advice. 25 million people work as independent professionals in the US alone... we like to say that they're all card-carrying members of guru.com... they just don't know it yet! And yes, there are also millions and millions of gurus abroad, in fact, we have gurus already registered for our service from 130 countries.

How is it unique?

We've created a brand that resonates with independent professionals and a service that empowers them to live and work the way they want. We believe that we understand and connect with our customers better than anyone else and that's what makes us special. We're solely focused on this business, and on empowering people who work on their own through our project marketplace, and our services to help them run their businesses.

What are your three top tips for building an Internet business?

1. Refuse to dilute your gene pool in your initial stages of building out your team. If you hire great people early, they will hire other talented and committed folks.
2. Don't take too long to perfect your site before getting it in front of your customers. Launch your site early, then learn from your customers. Ask them what's working and what's not and innovate rapidly.
3. Take more money rather than less money – company development cycles are so compressed these days and competition is so fierce... you may take a little more dilution up front, but you'll significantly increase your probability of being successful.

"At guru.com, we want to help change the way the world works. Guru.com is the leading online marketplace connecting expert freelancers and consultants (from virtual CEOs to graphic designers, and everything in between) with contract projects."

How did you secure finances?

We raised our first round of financing ($3m) from 20 individual angel investors – that's a lot of individual pitch meetings! The first few investors we landed were people we'd worked for in previous jobs – raise money from your former bosses – this is the best reference possible for other potential investors. We raised our second round of financing ($16m) from two Venture Capital firms called Greylock and August Capital.

Any advice for other start-ups?

Do everything you can to maximise the probability of being successful. Hire great people even if you have to give them more cash or equity, raise money from smart investors even if it dilutes you. Take a smaller piece of a bigger pie.

Golden opportunities

I would search out the golden opportunities of the future in quite similar fashion to the way we analysed opportunities when we started guru.com. I believe that great dot com business opportunities will exhibit a number of essential ingredients:

First, the product or service should emanate from your own personal experience or want. We founded guru.com because we had frustrating experiences trying to locate and contract with freelancers and consultants – word of mouth is inefficient - and saw lots of our friends and colleagues 'going guru'.

Second, the opportunity should emerge from a large market that is growing rapidly and that is supported by powerful broader societal/economic trends. In starting guru.com, we saw 25m people working on their own, and observed that the rise of information technology and shifting societal attitudes would continue to support this new way of working.

And third, I would focus on sectors with the potential to be redefined/enabled uniquely through harnessing the power of the Web. The guru.com project marketplace could not be effectively facilitated off-line.

How will you stay ahead?

First, by constantly asking our customers what they want, by listening to them and giving it to them. This is at the heart of most businesses, not just dot coms. Second, by spending a bit less time doing, and a bit more time thinking about our strategy and about how we evolve as a company. I'm going to spend more time looking out the window and thinking! It's important.

Personal hero

The customer service crew at guru.com. Actually, any person who does a great job in customer service at any dot com company. Seriously, they are the secret behind e-commerce.

Greatest thing about the Net

The efficiency of email – it makes it so much easier to communicate. The greater access to information enabled by the Web – there's just so much out there to explore.

Worst thing

The efficiency of email – it makes it so much easier to communicate (every time I clear out my email box it fills up again). The greater access to information enabled by the Web – there's just so much out there to explore. (Can be overwhelming sometimes and it sure is tough to hone in on what you want.)

Any quirks or interesting facts?

Black belt in Uechi Karate. 6'6" tall. Known to run around the halls of guru.com exclaiming "Can you feel it!" The momentum and energy, that is!

Other interests

Yoga – it's amazing, eye-opening, I love it. Wow am I inflexible though!
Listening to World music. Playing guitar – unfortunately, I'm just not all that good.
Squash – great workout in 45 minutes. Requires lots of strategic thought.

Friendly and accessible, well-structured and practical, Everywoman isn't just a complete departure from other woman-only portals but a personification of its founders, Karen Gill and Maxine Benson.

karen gill
maxine benson

Web liberators

everywoman.co.uk

For Karen Gill and Maxine Benson outstanding service in business is everything, which is why the Internet's reliability and convenience ensures the perfect delivery channel for their Everywoman website.

Everywoman.co.uk is brimming with all the useful information a woman could need, whether at home with children or on business. This includes a wealth of research material, inspiration, advice and networking opportunities. Friendly and accessible, yet practical and well-structured, Everywoman is a cyberworld away from the formal and inflexible corporate environments in which both Karen and Maxine spent the first 15 years of their careers. Moreover, through personifying the two directors, it's also a complete departure from other, rather patronising woman-only portals.

The story of how the partnership evolved started in the late 90s. Old friends, Karen and Maxine were keen to go into business together. However, they faced the perpetual challenges of limited access to information, restricted time and the simple need for someone with whom to share ideas and make contacts. It was a similar problem for no less than 80% of the market – women – who influenced 80% of buying decisions. Recognising a niche audience and specific need, they were convinced that the Internet held the key to reaching the market. So they collaborated to launch Everywoman, a UK-based online service specifically for British women.

Reasons to be cheerful

Their hunch returned handsome dividends. Today Karen and Maxine have every reason to be proud of Everywoman's success. The service, which has been online since September 1999, offers a direct access to a loyal and high-spending user base. Karen and Maxine have financed and managed the entire project by themselves, without the aid of big corporations who initially were happy to take copies of their business plan but less forthcoming with support or investment.

The partnership's continued determination not to play by the big boys' rules ensures that Karen and Maxine have a truly responsive and customer-focused service. Thanks to the site's innovative design, customers aren't simply part of an automated process. For example, all emails are answered personally. This level of flexibility promises other future benefits. Apart from personalising content Karen and Maxine can quickly develop new services in response to customer demand.

A fresh approach, an independent spirit

Mavericks to the core and keen to encourage refreshing alternatives to the bland, corporate Internet environment, Karen and Maxine are happy to pass on their advice to other start-ups. They also point out the pitfalls of operating in such a competitive and divisive industry.

"Firstly, move quickly and be very careful who you trust. Next, be realistic about your weaknesses and find the people with the skills to fill the gaps. Finally, don't be intimidated by the big boys – they don't always know best."

Delivering answers

Karen and Maxine hope to see a complete departure from the ageing processes that have governed the terrestrial business world for so long. They envisage a new business model specifically for the Internet, with faster decision-making processes, shorter development cycles and a culture of 'why not?' rather than 'why?'.

They appreciate that the Net is a great equaliser and that, in their own words, "the traditional problems of ageism, sexism and racism can be overcome on the Net. The Net can cut through class and cultural barriers and in time it will also cross socio-economic boundaries. There are no rules. Problems of speed and cost of access are already being addressed, once settled, anything is possible for anyone."

The Web's fabric of change

To Karen and Maxine the future of the Web offers services for all, not just today's privileged few. In their own words, the Internet will be 'everywhere and invisible', less a computer network, more a part of the very fabric of society. Similar to the Gold Rush of the 1800s, the opportunities will be there, not just for the online companies, but for the organisations who provide services, from website optimisation, design and hosting to product storage and delivery. In this spirit of openness, Karen and Maxine plan to build an inclusive community in which everyone has a voice and customers are treated not simply as one end of a transaction but partners, to be protected and rewarded.

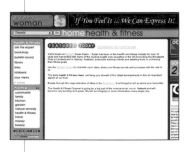

It comes as no surprise then, that Karen and Maxine name Candice Carpenter, founder of the iVillage site which first inspired them to create Everywoman as their dot com hero: "She has done an amazing job and most importantly, she's still doing it".

'Still doing it' sums up Karen and Maxine. Choosing 'never to give up' as their credo, they have proved the values that typify 21st-century femininity: independence, flexibility, and from a business perspective, an enthusiastic belief in great value-added service.

Thanks to the Web, Karen and Maxine are able to reach a global audience and so help ensure a better future for every woman, everywhere.

clicks & mortar

Pioneers going beyond traditional boundaries

Clicks & Mortar

Pioneers going beyond traditional boundaries

There is a new breed of manager in big business, individuals who are pioneering new ways of doing business, just like the Net Entrepreneurs. They have used the power of the Internet to change the way established companies operate, creating new business models. They are sharp and innovative, just like the founders of successful start-ups, but they face a different set of challenges, igniting change in a large traditional business. Established businesses have a history of being bureaucratic, risk averse and slow to make decisions (the average strategic investment decision taking over six months) – it takes guts, vision and charismatic leadership to challenge the rules.

They understand that the Internet is not an optional extra, and use it to deliver more to customers and make the Internet central to their business strategies. This new breed of managers have put their companies at the leading edge. With vision and self belief these people have created new divisions, new products and services, creating shareholder value based on the Internet without anyone else showing them.

The days of consensus management have gone, by being more open, direct and making decisions fast. The key is not to be cautious and back a well-defined idea, many of them took risks and could not predict the future. Mike Harris of Egg certainly did not know that he was going to achieve his five-year business targets in six months.

In the majority, these heroes began their careers in traditional businesses. Mike Harris of Egg was originally Chief Executive of Prudential. Paul Barry-Walsh was Head of Safetynet Plc, the disaster recovery company before launching NetStore. The companies themselves, from Hilton and Nokia to Victor Chandler and Electronic Telegraph, have their roots in the old world. Handbag.com is a joint venture between the Boots Group and the New Media division of the Telegraph Publishing Group. Eventures is a joint venture between Softbank and ePartners, an Internet Venture Capitalist backed by News Corporation. Without exception, these heroes have backbone as well as substance as these initiatives demonstrate.

Business boundaries are blurring, successful businesses everywhere are Internet-centric. Successful dot com start-ups and big business have the same characteristics, they act Internet time, put the customer first and operate by new rules. They both also recognise the power and strength of forging alliances and strategic partnerships and increasingly partner with each other, there is a great synergy in combining the assets and resources of a large business with the innovative new ideas of a dot com business.

The Internet, extranets, intranets, they all improve efficiency, productivity communication, service and reduce costs. Combining this with the tangible assets of bricks and mortar is the future of business. Bricks to clicks entrepreneurs have the benefit of access to huge resources and brand equity. Combining these resources with a dot com vision and a new management style has propelled major companies forward and is not optional for any company.

Yet, by the same token, these are the companies and the people who saw the opportunities of the Internet and its application for their businesses. While many considered the Internet simply as a technology to make the existing business operate better, with intranets, for example, or email, these heroes took the concept to a whole new level. They created new, Internet-focused ventures, such as BT Cellnet's Genie, which gives customers a wealth of information services from their mobile phone.

What distinguishes these heroes is, as Hugo Drayton of Hollinger Telegraph New Media described, "the unique combination of cool professionalism and get-ahead zest". They have taken an existing concept, such as gaming, media or software, and given it a whole new spin. Take Paul Barry-Walsh at NetStore. What differentiates his service is not so much his software for distributed enterprises, but the way it is delivered and managed – over the Internet. As a result, his customers enjoy "the kind of power and flexibility normally unavailable to small to middle size companies". Likewise, Brian Greasley at Genie describes his brief as leading the development of fixed and mobile Internet convergence. They're creating something that is more than the sum of its parts and universally agree that funding is essential in order to achieve it to the necessary degree of quality.

Hugo Drayton – Hollinger Telegraph
New Media

So, while traditional business values, such as market research to understand customers, strategic planning, funding and management, still hold, this new breed of heroes has the adventurous spirit of the Internet age. While they have responsibilities to meet, business plans to write and shareholders to satisfy, they are still in a position to experiment and take risks. Throw away the rule book, they urge.

As far as the Clicks & Mortar heroes are concerned, the Internet business model exists in its own right, it is more than just another channel. It has a new set of rules and these are the people with the luxury of freedom and resources to make them. Egg, for example, is completely distinct from Prudential, with its own management team, board and structures and can as a result be more flexible and make decisions faster than a cumbersome traditional business.

Brian Greasley – Genie

They are also pragmatic about what makes a website succeed. It must be easy to find and intuitive to use, it must deliver information and services quickly and efficiently, with customer-focused content and a strong proposition. As Hugo Drayton warns, just because a service or product is available on the Net doesn't automatically make it desirable. "Don't assume that everyone will rush to the Web, it will only work if we make people's lives easier and more fun". He is convinced, and his Clicks & Mortar compatriots agree, that value for money, customer service and branding are more important than ever in an Internet environment. Dominic Riley of handbag.com, for his part, advises that the quality of the implementation is as important, or more so, than identifying the niche.

When delivering these services, many of the heroes have recognised the benefit of outsourcing the delivery of the technology architecture. Rob Wilmot of Freeserve partnered with Planet Online allowing him to focus on the business strategy.

Rob Wilmot – Dixons Freeserve

The future for these new heroes is bright. They have the agility and responsiveness of a start-up, yet enjoy the security and firm foundations of a traditional business. They have the confidence of well-researched good ideas, but the passion to keep striving to expand the horizons of their imaginations.

With a clear vision
of 'we are on the
customer's side',
Mike Harris, Chief
Executive, has turned
the industry on its head
and beat the company's
five-year targets in
just six months with Egg,
the Web-based financial
services company.

mike harris

Online banking supremo

As far as Mike Harris, head of Egg, is concerned, the Internet is secondary to his real passion – placing customers first and foremost. Service is his primary concern and technology is simply the means. Introduction of latest technology is of value to Egg only if it leads to satisfying and attracting new customers.

At the time he became Chief Executive of Prudential in 1995, Mike envisaged the Internet facility as a telephone banking service with a website. He felt that the Web wouldn't provide enough critical mass. At best it would simply be a secondary, supporting channel to the telephone service.

And then, upon Egg being launched in October 1998, the Internet as a medium exploded, catapulting the Prudential's service into the stratosphere. Targets aimed at acquiring five million customers and £5bn in deposits in five years were accomplished in just six months. A truly remarkable achievement masterminded by Mike.

An agent for the customer, not the industry

Such an astounding success wasn't simply due to being in the right place at the right time. It was due to Prudential's advanced application of technology via the Web, replacing in its entirety hitherto traditional financial services. The results speak for themselves. As Mike says, "Our vision is very clear. We are on the customer's side. We position ourselves as the customer's agent in managing their money and their lives". Consequently, the vast majority of customers acknowledge Egg as a distinctive and worthy brand, refreshingly honest, completely consistent and open about its mistakes.

The listening bank...

Mike carries this customer-focused approach to extremes. He gives out his personal email address and invites customers to contact him. He also advocates the benefits of using the Web and, bearing in mind Egg's reputation for clarity, regards himself duty bound to make the introduction of Web technology simple and straightforward.

A separate business, a fresh approach, a new model

Although owned 100% by the Prudential, Egg serves the market as a separate entity, with its own management team and structures, its own board and values. Exercising such autonomy, Egg is completely divorced from the constraints and traditions of past marketing concepts. Customers rely on Egg to give instant and expert response to financial needs.

Mike has the rare talent of listening to customers and, if within the scope of Egg, satisfying them.

Egg might be far away in Cyberspace, but it's close to customers.

Hugo Drayton, Managing Director of Hollinger Telegraph New Media (owners of Electronic Telegraph – the UK's first online national newspaper), is one of the UK's leading authorities on new media, a champion of content and a vigorous defender of on-site registration.

hugo drayton

E-media mogul

telegraph.co.uk

Everyone talks about 'Internet time' as a recent phenomenon. Return to the summer of 1994 and Hugo Drayton was already racing ahead at speeds that, by the standards of the day, seemed practically supersonic. Having joined the *Daily Telegraph* and been given a brief to develop a weekly electronic newspaper, Hugo realised that customers wouldn't wait that long. They needed the news instantly – not weekly.

It's a measure of Hugo's dedication and commitment that, in an industry especially cautious about launching new products, he managed to convince an incredulous board that a daily national online newspaper, the first of its kind, was the way forward. This at a time when there was no indication that the Web would become an important part of the media industry. However, Hugo's lobbying paid off and his assurances were well founded. Within a day of launching Electronic Telegraph, they had blown out the capacity of the 64-megabyte line, award followed award and the rest is history.

Part classic English gent, part sharp-eyed entrepreneur

Today, Hugo is considered one of the UK's leading authorities on new media. He is gifted with a rare combination of cool professionalism and fervent expertise that embodies the best of Clicks & Mortar. He possesses the technology knowledge and talent to spot a good idea and stick by it. Despite criticism he has vigorously defended the concept of on-site registration for visitors. Considering the massive value that registration provides in terms of marketing, and hence, profiling data, his intuition not only proved correct but also is paying him a dividend.

Hugo is a man who has put the lessons gained during his distinguished online career to good use. "Have a niche and stick to it" is his advice to start-up businesses. "Remember, it's a global world and so versatile. Do not absorb too many ideas at the same time. Concentrate on one project at a time like QXL. Commitment is an essential ingredient for online success. This includes ensuring you have the right level of commitment from your team."

From walled garden to open market

Hugo considers content to be the cornerstone of any information-led online service. At first, Electronic Telegraph was a self-contained service. Yet, Hugo soon came to accept the need to link to other sites. Now a team of 60 backs the Electronic Telegraph site, of whom almost half are editors: an explicit indication of the importance of content. Hugo also stresses the importance of preparation and research whilst recommending would-be dot com heroes to concentrate on areas they are passionate about. He warns, "Stick to your core competencies, be brutal about avoiding faddish distractions".

Never forget the real world

Hugo emphasises that just because a service or product is available online, it doesn't automatically become attractive or desirable. Traditional business ethics, such as offering value for money and customer service, have become more important than ever. He advises, "Be ruthless about seeing your product from the customer's viewpoint. Don't assume that everyone will rush to the Web. It will only work if we make people's lives easier and more fun".

Senior Vice President of IT
at Hilton International,
Nigel Underwood lives out
the company's Web
values of 'Winning, Ethical
and Balanced.' They're
what drives him to create
the perfect virtual
organisation to offer
Hilton guests the best
possible service and
value for money.

nigel underwood

When did you first get involved in the Net?

Hilton.com was founded in 1995. I didn't join Hilton International until mid-1997 at which stage we re-visited our business and systems strategies and agreed the direction based on four phases of activity:

1. We needed a global infrastructure – a firm foundation on which to build 'Competitive Advantage Through Systems'.
2. To ensure our line of business systems were all Year 2000 compliant.
3. To focus on our customer facing systems – to change the emphasis from hotel management to customer management.
4. To deliver a global integrated business – built on 'organisational and locational flexibility'.

Since 1997, phase 4 has guided our vision to invest in a limited number of global IT vendors with a common vision of the future for integrated systems delivered via the Web. To date we have achieved phases 1 and 2 globally and phase 3 in parts of the Hilton world. If phase 4 has driven the 'what' we're trying to deliver, our values have driven the 'how' so similarly in '97 we agreed across the systems team the 'WEB' would also be our values:

W – Winning (being first, best etc).
E – Ethical (being honest, trusting etc).
B – Balanced (achieving an equilibrium with our family lives, treating suppliers as partners etc).

What is your greatest achievement?

Yet to come! All great hotels are built on firm foundations (but to date no-one has built a hotel top to bottom with clicks). 2000 will be the year in which Hilton International truly opens our doors to the public and trading partners alike.

Key behind site

Our brand is the number one hospitality brand. It stands for quality, for service, for innovation, for security. We will continue to strive to align our systems and Web presence with these very same values. If we fall short we will devalue the brand, if we succeed we will grow Hilton's reputation and pre-eminence as one of the world's leading brands.

How is it unique?

As above plus our partners help to ensure our systems deliver to promise – they're world class – Sun for hardware, Oracle for database and our back office applications, Compaq to provide support and Fidelio/Rezsolutions for our industry specific applications.

What are your three top tips for building an Internet business?

1. A passion for understanding and exceeding the specific needs of each and every consumer/customer – using information intelligently and in a 'trusted' way for the benefit of the consumer.
2. A commitment to developing/growing a quality brand built on 100% execution to promise through the organisation's processes and people.
3. A great team of people bonded through a common purpose and set of values with confidence in their own ability.

How did you secure finances?

Hilton International funds and contributing to the alliance's investment alongside HHC. We're 'experimenting', however, with novel approaches such as incubator.com (why not think and act like a start-up!)

Any advice for other start-ups?

Be clear about vision and objectives. Do your homework on the market and really understand customer needs. Get some quality external input (non execs, partners who can help.) Don't give away (or even sell!) the crown jewels. Retain focus/nudge the steering wheel frequently but go fast, go boldly, go now!

Advice for a traditional business
Get the best CIO and keep him or her!

Your vision of the Web's future
"What We Want" (not What Went Wrong). As a businessman, to ensure that our customers, shareholders, suppliers and employees are delighted with the way in which our firm uses it to it's full potential. Specifically, as a CIO to apply it (but hide it!) as a fundamental component of our architecture to deliver the perfect virtual organisation. To ensure that a Hilton guest gets the best quality of service and the best value for money. Also that our service providers be they employees or suppliers have the knowledge, processes and tools to deliver what they need effectively and enjoyably and that our shareholders get excellent returns from the investments. As a citizen to achieve the above two things in harmony for the benefit of our children (and wives) everywhere.

Golden opportunities
Too many to list!

How will you stay ahead?
Vision, passion, investment, speed, experimentation, execution.

Any Net predictions?
The gap will grow – great global brands will partner with great global brands and their share price will continue to escalate. The people who run or invest in these great global brands will have more money and the wise ones more time!

Personal hero
Jeff Bezos – he has the vision and passion to lead the way. I thank him on behalf of the industry and the customer, for lighting the fires and showing other more established businesses the way ahead.

Favourite sites
redimps.com, claricecliff.com, blueuu.com

Greatest thing about the Net
As a consumer to get information on what I want whenever I want or wherever I am. As the majority shareholder in Nigel Underwood plc, the Web offers the opportunity and choice to strike the balance and score goals for my organisation, its customers and suppliers. As a father, it's the future for my children's education and careers.

Worst thing
It's still not intuitive enough. It's slow and sometimes unreliable – give me a tap or a dial tone. It's synonymous still with the 'T' rather than the 'I' in IT – the tangible versus the intangible – with jargon such as URLs, cookies, portals...! Everyone's an expert – promises of a life of ice cream and after dinner mints!

What inspires you?
People. My parents. They had little but gave me the chance and the desire. My wife Anne gives me support and guidance. My children have the passion to make a difference.

What should inspire others?
Whatever is most important in their lives.

Soundbite
'Why do you always phone when the Archers is on' – my wife almost every evening! 'CATS – Competitive Advantage Through Systems'. 'One Hilton, One team, Number One'.

Other interests
Spending time with my family – I have four children (Matthew, Clarice, Zak and John). Watching Lincoln City play football, Particularly singing 'Winter Wonderland' accompanied by Ringo and the band. Humming loudly alongside the air-raid siren at corners and impersonating the Dambusters after we've scored!

> "Be clear about vision and objectives. Do your homework on the market and really understand customer needs."

Drew Kaza, Managing
Director of Internet
and Interactive for
BBC Worldwide, has
entertainment running in
his veins. The commercial
BBC site prides itself on
more than 8 million hits
a month.

drew kaza

Widecast entrepreneur

bbc.com/beeb.com

Making careful decisions based on a variety of factors and information is the key to successful betting. According to Victor Chandler, creator of the most customer-friendly betting site on the Web, research is also a critical success factor in an online enterprise.

When did you first get involved in the Net?
1997.

What is your greatest achievement?
Going live on 16th January 2000.

Key behind site
A site which will be the most customer-friendly betting site on the Web.

What are your three top tips for building an Internet business?
1. Platform and engine function.
2. Research of market.
3. Research where you are going to get your customers from.

How did you secure finances?
Owned existing business.

How will you stay ahead?
Planning long-term strategy and investing in technology.

Any Net predictions?
Bigger and better.

Personal hero
Simon Ordish who works for me.

Favourite sites
amazon.com and iAuctions.

Greatest thing about the Net
Saves on petrol and shoe leather.

Worst thing
Speed.

What inspires you?
Success.

victor chandler

Ahead of the game

victorchandler.com

Photo – Gerry Cranham

Any advice for other start-ups?
Research of market.

Advice for a traditional business
Get moving.

Your vision of the Web's future
Worldwide growth.

Golden opportunities
Too numerous to name.

What should inspire others?
Other people's success.

Any quirks or interesting facts?
I could not turn on a computer a year ago.

Other interests
My horses.

Decisive yet relaxed,
Dominic Riley, Managing
Director, is famous for
identifying opportunities
and taking action on
them. This is, after all, the
man who took Handbag,
the UK's leading portal for
women, online just 12
weeks after the launch.

dominic riley

Web business equaliser

handbag.com

"I recognise the important things and get them done," is how Dominic Riley, Managing Director of handbag.com, chooses to describe the essence of his business philosophy.

Grasping opportunities and pursuing them have been the overriding principles driving Dominic's career. They are also the key reasons for the phenomenal success of handbag.com.

Back when email was young – and green
Dominic first confronted email – admittedly an early, green screen version of the technology – whilst on an MBA studies exchange visit to Austin, Texas. Dominic soon recognised the potential of this revolutionary form of communication – particularly as a handy way to stay in touch with Debbie, his future wife. This early encounter with the Internet was to sow the seeds for Dominic's distinguished online career.

From strategy to service in just 12 weeks
In 1997, after a short time at Kingfisher, Dominic was given the role of Head of Marketing at BBC Online. Whilst there he helped to turn bbc.com into Europe's most popular website. His greatest achievement followed, taking the women-only portal handbag.com online just 12 weeks after joining as employee number one.

Handbag.com is an outstanding example of Dominic's rare talent to turn opportunity into reality. Though it was generally accepted that women constituted the fastest growing online group and were responsible for 75% of purchasing decisions, those two facts had failed to be linked commercially. To the chagrin of many wannabes, handbag.com exploited the market gap successfully through its wealth of features targeted specifically at women.

Handbag.com features far more than an approachable design and dynamic, daily changing content. The portal has backbone as well as substance, which is based on a long term 50% joint venture between the Boots Group and the New Media division of the Telegraph Publishing Group. Philosophically, Dominic points out that "while good ideas are useful, without action, support and strategy they are worthless".

Edited content, interactivity and 'every day different'
Two features differentiate handbag.com from other Web enterprises: targeting and dynamism. "One size portals are plentiful," points out Dominic. "For example many leading brands in food and drink, beauty and gardening provide content. Likewise, it is relatively easy to create a static website. Handbag.com has moved a stage further."

It provides edited, expert content for a specific audience. Whilst its 'every day different' ethos offers a fresh experience with every visit, handbag.com's interactivity enables visitors to tailor that experience via inputting personal details. So they gain a personalised surfing experience and the portal accrues valuable business intelligence.

Leaping towards success

Dominic recommends this approach to anyone developing an online service. "Focused implementation is as important, if not more so, than identifying the niche," advises Dominic. "Organising the right team, having deep pockets and the capacity to improve the service" are Dominic's suggested ingredients to turn opportunities into profit.

"In other words, action opens doors in today's fast-moving, competitive Internet arena." Dominic is bemused by traditional business people who spend more time talking about the potential of the Internet than doing anything about it. "Less navel gazing and more getting on with it," is his tip. "You'll learn more by doing than by thinking about doing".

"Two years ago, when the market was still in its infancy online ventures could make mistakes and survive. Now both stakes and expectations have accelerated at an incredible pace. High entry costs and an ever increasing crowded market mean that businesses will be at a serious disadvantage if they don't get online quickly."

A colourful prediction in black and white

Despite handbag.com's superb quality, Dominic confesses to sometimes feeling like "John Logie Baird demonstrating an early television, with a fuzzy black and white picture and crackly sound. Relatively speaking, the Internet is still in its first incarnation. One day we'll laugh at the slow speed of websites and clumsy online services we once thought were cutting-edge".

Dominic visualises a future where segmentation will be as advanced as technology. "There will be more portals for more sectors of the community, with targeted services for specific groups, including children, teenagers, people working at home and many more."

Business rules the Net

A businessman at heart, Dominic's dotcom heroes are those who have achieved a commercial success with the Internet. He admires David Filo and Jerry Yang, the two founders of Yahoo! and their textbook backroom-to-billionaire story. Similarly, Ellen Pack, the brilliant businesswoman and founder of women.com in the USA.

Dominic would like to go down in history not so much as a great visionary or guru, but, "as someone who used the Web to enhance womens' lives and to make money".

When it comes to adding up Internet assets, it all equals business to Dominic Riley.

"Focused implementation is as important, if not more so, than identifying the niche."

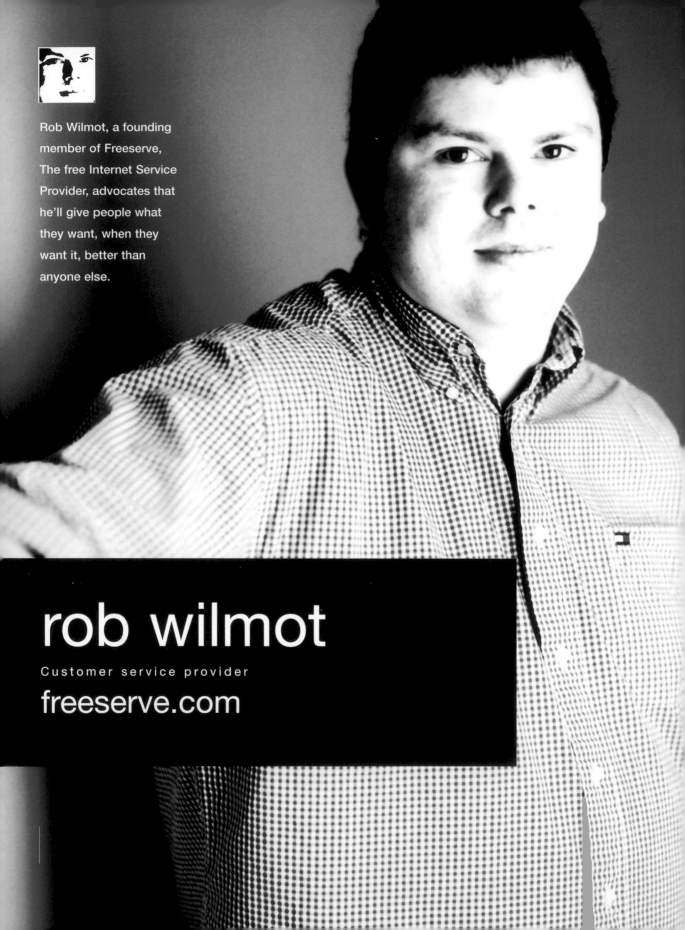

When did you first get involved in the Net?

Back in 1995 when working for a cable company. I got the company connected to the Internet with email. I then moved to join an Internet start-up called Planet Online Ltd where I became Web Master. I moved into consultancy from there.

What is your greatest achievement?

Being involved with taking Freeserve from a Limited Company to a Plc in seven months. That alone was fantastic, but building a team and infrastructure to support such a venture was where the real magic happened.

Key behind site

Simple proposition/quality service.

How is it unique?

Freeserve was the first fully featured free ISP; what differentiates us from our competition now is the quality and depth of service found on the Freeserve portal.

What are your three top tips for building an Internet business?

1. Keep it simple. Get your message across quickly and clearly. You may have the simplest product on the Net, but unless you explain it in easy terms on your site, people will go elsewhere.
2. Marketing. Get your site known and get traffic to it: traffic = customers. Effective marketing can begin with getting yourself listed in the right search engines, right through to a slick banner ad campaign.
3. Get your technology and infrastructure right. If your site is too busy that no one can get to it because your servers cannot cope, or you cannot fulfil an order because of ill thought out logistics, your business will not last long in an ever growing competitive market.

How did you secure finances?

Our parent company were quick to identify the opportunity. Investment came from there.

Any advice for other start-ups?

Do your research – the best Web ideas are simple and although there may already be someone on the Net already doing something the same or similar, this doesn't stop you doing it better!

Identify a need – one of my favourite examples of this is lastminute.com. They had the idea that many people were too busy to go through the trouble of finding a holiday, and that such people were more likely to look for last-minute deals on the spur of the moment. Just add Internet and 'hey presto' a Net success story.

Raise funding – you've had your great idea to become the next dot com success but you need more than your limited finances to make your concept fly. You'll need some Venture Capital. VC funds have become the *de facto* standard for raising money and many have sprung up over the last year. Firsttuesday.com is a site which brings people with good ideas together with those who have money to invest.

Advice for a traditional business

There's a product or service on the Internet which will have the same effect as a bullet with your company's name on it. Get a bullet-proof jacket for your business by formulating an e-commerce strategy.

Register your domain name before someone else does

Get someone who knows what they are talking about to help you get started. Depending on your size and investment capability, this might be one of the traditional blue chip consulting firms. Equally, the Internet is such an entrepreneurial space at the moment, that the consultant who is most suitable to help you, is working from her spare bedroom. Whatever you do, choose your advice wisely.

Your vision of the Web's future

In his book Neuromancer, William Gibson described cyberspace as a holistic virtual world where people interact seemlessly with data.

This is how I see the future of the Web: another data/information channel which will converge, collectively, with other media and information type, and be displayed to people based on a set of user defined rules. Combine this with Articifical Intelligence systems and you'll get into your car and it will give you a weather update based on GPS data. You'll see that it is going to be icy on the roads. Your car will then tell you that the tread on your tyres is dangerously low and that you should order new tyres for the winter. Knowing your preference for Pirelli tyres you car will automatically display the four nearest garages that have Pirelli tyres in stock with a price comparison. You will say out loud your preference for option four and will be asked if you want to make the debit from your current account which will be checked for available funds should you make the purchase.

In short, the Internet will form part of a vast but intuitive personalised information matrix which is truly device and location agnostic.

How will you stay ahead?

By giving people what they want, when they want it, better than anybody else.

Any Net predictions?

One day, every business, every public service, everybody will be touched by the Net.

Personal hero

Personal: My girlfriend, for putting up with me working every waking dot com hour to make Freeserve a success – and for her persistence in stealing time with me.
Professional: Ajaz Ahmed, of Freeserve, for his e-commerce market vision.

Favourite sites

Besides the freeserve.com portal;
ukinvest.co.uk
dilbert.com
nasa.org.uk

Greatest thing about the Net
Having the potential to find everything you want at your fingtertips.

Worst thing
The amount of thinking time I dedicate to it.

What inspires you?
Blazing a trail alongside similarly motivated colleagues.

What should inspire others?
Whatever makes you get out of bed in the morning and bore people at parties.

Soundbite
If you asked my Mum: 'He works with computers'.
If you ask my girlfriend: 'He works on the Internet'.
If you ask my PA: 'He's busy but I can get you in next Thursday'.

Any quirks or interesting facts?
A parable about the power of the Internet:

Back in 1997, I was responsible for building the Leeds United Football Club website for a venture that later became Sports Internet.

We were doing a live audio broadcast, taking the feed from LUFC's local radio station (which was essentially a mobile studio in the back of a van in the car park behind the stand). The radio station's terrestrial license only permitted it to broadcast within a ten mile radius of the football stadium. During half time it was customary for the radio station to run a competition. Imagine my delight when the first caller identified himself as Chris from Christchurch, New Zealand. He was listening to the match on the Internet. This was made more poignant as he said that there was no other way that he could get live coverage from any other traditional TV/Satellite or radio channel in NZ.

Chris won the competition and bought a replica strip from the online store.This was when I fundamentally understood that the future of the Net would be big!

Other interests
I am an exhibiting artist – contemporary portraiture – big canvases – big brush strokes. Keen guitarist. Driving through the Scottish Highlands with the roof down.

Like everyone else, I am writing a book.

> "Raise funding – you've had your great idea to become the next dot com success but you need more than your limited finances to make your concept fly. You'll need some Venture Capital. VC funds have become the *de facto* standard for raising money and many have sprung up over the last year."

Bob Head, CEO of Smile, is the man behind the first UK bank to offer free internet banking. This was just the start of his 'built to last' innovative strategies.

bob head

Smiling all the way to the bank

smile.co.uk

When did you first get involved in the Net?
1998 Egg.

What is your greatest achievement?
Switching Egg from a telephone business model to an Internet business model.

Key behind site
Passion.

How is it unique?
First Internet bank in the UK but that is not enough for the future. Watch this space.

What are your three top tips for building an Internet business?
Care – to get it done awesomely. Don't care – to get some sleep. Have fun – because it's a tough environment. Be passionate about the customer.

How did you secure finances?
From the Co-Operative bank.

Any advice for other start-ups?
A good idea used to be good enough but the world is changing fast and you need more than a good idea. Now you need a well thought through business model.

Advice for a traditional business
Tolerate the mavericks and get them into action.

Your vision of the Web's future
We are about 5% in to what is possible. The 95% is unknown so a vision is difficult, except it will be awesome.

Golden opportunities
Develop true brands which means that propositions will be centred on other things than just price.

How will you stay ahead?
True brand values, passion and total focus on the customer.

Any Net predictions?
The guys with one good idea will be swallowed up or fail. The get rich share option companies will be seen for what they are. The 'built to last, not built to list' companies will win out. Also watch out for the co-operative organisations. The Internet is ideal for this type of business.

Personal hero
Amazon.

Favourite Sites
zappa.com, cdnow.com, uk8.multimaps.com, egg.com, motleyfool.com, f1rumors.net, thehungersite.com, smile.co.uk.

Greatest thing about the Net
Right here, right now, wherever, whenever, whatever.

Worst thing
Spam.

What inspires you?
People in general – I think there is greatness in everyone though sometimes it is hard to see or liberate it. My Auntie Min is probably the greatest person I know.

What should inspire others?
Nothing should inspire other people and anything could. If you can get all the emotions, feelings and beliefs of an organisation hooked up and aligned with the brand, then that would be an inspired organisation.

Soundbite
The art of diplomacy is letting other people have your way.

Any quirks or interesting facts?
The list is dangerous, probably best to stay silent.

Other interests?
Snooker, cycling, music and messing about.

Brian Greasley, Managing Director of the Genie Internet service which provides Net-based information to customers' Cellnet mobile phones, believes that the Net is like a treasure hunt and "you have to get to the clues faster than the other guy". With Genie, that's exactly what he has done.

When did you first get involved in the Net?
I first became involved in the Internet in 1986, when I started scoping how the Internet could be integrated into mobile phones.

What is your greatest achievement?
Inventing Genie Internet.

Key behind site
The key is to provide a single Internet site that is designed to provide lifestyle services wherever you are.

How is it unique?
It is the only site of its kind in the country and it's leading the development of fixed and mobile Internet convergence and as such its customers benefit from some of the most advanced services in the UK.

Any advice for other start-ups?
I believe that start-ups need to secure sufficient funding in the first round, need to ensure that they are investing at least 20% of their budget in marketing and have the strength of character to focus on the big things.

Advice for a traditional business
Worry.

Your vision of the Web's future
I believe that the Internet currently does less than 10% of what it is capable of and will evolve to be a life tool. It will wake you when it knows your train is late and you have to drive, it will be with you 24hrs a day and there will be more mobiles on the Internet worldwide than PCs within three years.

brian greasley

Mobile treasure hunter

genie.co.uk

What are your three top tips for building an Internet business?
1. Do it now.
2. Create a separate organisation to do it – it's not business as usual.
3. Throw away the old rule book.

How did you secure finances?
I secured funding from the board of BT Cellnet, based on a number of presentations and a business plan.

Golden opportunities
Mobile Internet
Capturing personal data – diaries, address books etc
Gambling
Kid's portal sites

How will you stay ahead?

We will stay ahead because we will continue to take more risks than our competitors – we will re-invent ourselves every three months and we will continue to live and breath what we do.

Any Net predictions?

One billion mobile phones on the Internet by 2003. 600m PCs by 2003 hence mobile and mobile devices are the dominant platform.

Personal hero

Andreesen – he was on the verge of using it to re-invent the status quo.

Favourite sites

nasdaq.com
dobedo.com
pepsi.com

Greatest thing about the Net

Anyone can do something on it.

Worst thing

Everyone can do something on it.

What inspires you?

My wife, my children and a belief that anything is possible.

What should inspire others?

A belief that anything is possible.

Soundbite

The Internet is like a treasure hunt. No one knows the answer you just have to get to the clues faster than the other guy.

Any quirks or interesting facts?

I am dyslexic.

Other interests

Lots...

"I believe that the Internet currently does less than 10% of what it is capable of and will evolve to be a life tool."

One of the world's top brands, Richard Branson's collection of businesses is set to be one of the leading internet brands, from virgin.com the leading portal site, to Virgin Net one of the top 3 UK ISPs.

richard branson

Virgin king

virgin.com

It's almost 40 years since the founder of one of the world's most universally acclaimed brands first sealed his mark. From his school days, knowingly or unknowingly, Richard Branson's talent was destined for 'bigger things'. He first successfully ran a student magazine. The Internet was unheard of, so his working hours were mainly confined to setting up deals via the telephone. He recalls, "I had to become an entrepreneur to deal with the advertising and paper manufacturers. Learning the art of survival took up more time than learning the art of editing a magazine".

Along with his colleagues, Richard then ventured into the commercially unknown to set up a record company. After days of discussion they settled on the name Virgin. It sounded trendy and, as Richard said at the time, "We could apply it to other businesses, not just music" .

An endless stream of other enterprises followed the record label. Today, 96% of British consumers have heard of Virgin, which has established itself, as one of the world's top 50 brands. The brand's reputation is so extensive that it is even acclaimed in countries where it doesn't even trade. Richard Branson's empire embraces 340 different businesses and joint ventures, producing a total worldwide revenue in excess of £3bn (US$5bn).

If the Web fits...

Virgin's entry into the Web is the latest strategic piece of a corporate jigsaw that completes the circle of Richard's uncanny ability to view the global marketplace as a 'big picture'. It's perfect for e-commerce – a ready-made cyber-conglomerate waiting to be linked. "Suddenly the Internet comes along and I am able to say the last thirty years was a carefully crafted plan," quips Richard.

Web-wide open

Richard plans to secure a pole position for Virgin in digital Britain's technologies marketplace. He's investing heavily in Virgin Group's website, virgin.com – solidly establishing itself first in Britain and expanding worldwide. From the site, Richard will sell consumers everything from cars and CDs to wedding dresses, electricity and much more besides.

Virgin.com is just one of Richard's multi-faceted Web enterprises. Plans are afoot to turn it into one of the world's top portal sites.

With over 800,000 subscribers, Richard's Virgin Net already ranks among the top three Internet Service Providers in the UK. It offers not just free Internet access but also cogent scope that includes entertainment and leisure services, holiday bookings news and reviews as well as music gig guides. These facilities are just the beginning. Eventually, virgin.com will create a link that lets customers bargain shop among Virgin's competitors before they buy. Richard is gearing up to launch four to six stand-alone Net businesses every six weeks.

"New businesses joining the Web will definitely benefit from the start. They will discover ways and means to save on overheads. Some companies can do it in a much bigger way than others. Obviously with our Virgin brand and its worldwide reputation, it would be madness for us not to try and be one of the top ten portals on a global basis."

On the move

Virgin Mobile, which sells phones, is on target to sign up just under one million customers before 2001. Virgin phones offers "no complicated monthly talk plans or tariffs. No fixed term contract to sign with scandalous monthly charges. Just simple pricing, great service and a whole range of other standard options".

These include: free voicemail, text messaging, international roaming, caller display, call waiting, fax and data, Virgin Net CD and a phone book manager. The company will also play a key part in Richard's venture into the Wireless Application Protocol (WAP) mobile Internet arena. By 2002 Europe's e-commerce revenues are expected to exceed $223bn. And Richard plans to deliver his Web offering not only through PCs but also through his cell-phone ventures.

He also plans to offer cellular services on the Continent. His ultimate objective is to run his own network in the UK, and consolidate the service even farther afield. It has been estimated that Virgin will bid an estimated $800m for new British mobile licenses, with the backing of names like George Soros and Microsoft Co-founder Paul Allen. (Bidding for European licenses is already in progress.)

The business choice

Until now, the average small business had found that establishing a Web presence involved a string of convoluted factors. Web pages as such present no problem, most businesses opt for a free dial-up account and a post-for hosted website, which is invariably based in the US. But securing payment protocols is costly. If a business wants a credit card merchant account extended to the Web, it may have to wait months for it to materialise, coupled with a premium on the bank percentage charges for the privilege of doing so.

Richard's Biznet dispenses altogether with such a complicated and costly procedure. Biznet also helps businesses achieve a sturdy Web presence from a standard website to one capable of secure online e-commerce 24 hours a day, seven days a week.

Getting cars onto the superhighway

The British consumer has voted with his feet by walking away from higher than average European costs for cars. Recognising this exodus, Virgin cars promises to sell leading brand name cars direct to the UK consumer via the Web, 24-7. Richard promises a 'fair and honest' approach which is in keeping with his already highly successful Virgin mobile phones deal.

In both instances the company promises no confusing marketing ploys. This typifies Richard's belief that the Web should be accessible to all.

Richard is convinced that eventually every British company will have a Web presence, simply to survive. He maintains, "New businesses joining the Web will definitely benefit from the start. They will discover ways and means to save on overheads. Some companies can do it in a much bigger way than others. Obviously with our Virgin brand and its worldwide reputation, it would be madness for us not to try and be one of the top ten portals on a global basis".

Completing the picture

Collectively, Richard's cyber-conglomorate jigsaw pieces could be worth as much as £4bn ($6.5bn). He doesn't altogether rule out an initial public offering or either his share of Virgin Airlines or his Net businesses. But an IPO isn't a priority. He prefers keeping his companies private, selling off chunks when he needs cash. The Singapore Airlines contract is a good example whereby he acquired $979m, for investment into his Internet ventures.

What really completes the picture is that Richard embodies the passion and entrepreneurial spirit of the Internet. He has always done business based on his own rules, his open philosophy and personality.

He is the original hero who has embraced dot com.

"Suddenly the Internet comes along and I am able to say the last thirty years was a carefully crafted plan," quips Richard.

38-year-old Managing
Director, Michael Foster
is behind the success of
the online business portal,
FT.com which boasts 2.5
million members.

michael foster

Global business news magnate

FT.com

The dot com hero behind the redevelopment of the *Financial Times* website FT.com into a highly sophisticated global business portal is Michael Foster aged 38, its Managing Director. He is dynamic, enthusiastic and in his own words, "Very driven. I like to get on with it. My inspiration comes from working with a great team and making things happen."

Taking such a powerful brand and redeveloping its website into a global business portal is an ambitious undertaking, especially in a timeframe of just seven months. Michael previously worked as a media and telecommunications consultant at Reuters using his talent making deals and putting news on Yahoo! during a period when the Web was still in its early stages.

At the Financial Times, with the backing of 100 journalists, Michael succeeded in transforming FT.com, focusing on improved content and functionality. "My first task was to quickly re-design the existing FT.com website and market it aggressively, while simultaneously concentrating on overall redevelopment. This cumulated in the launch of the global business portal in February 2000."

The backbone behind the site

The upgraded site provides new design and navigation functionality, enabling easy manoeuvrability to any part of the site. Latest features include office tools such as personal email, file storage and an online diary; extensive discussion forums around key business topics; new dossiers about key people in business; career advice and resources; powerful new ways to search the Web for business and carefully selected shopping and services options. At the heart of FT.com is constantly updated news, analysis and market prices. All these facilities are powered by new technology with hardware and software provided by talented technology partners.

Michael explains further, "My primary aim is for the new FT.com to become the leading Internet resource for business people everywhere, helping them to make sense of a complex, rapidly changing world. We want to place international business people within one click of the package of resources available to further their interests. Our core strengths are content and brand. We outsource all our IT needs, largely to American best-in-class Internet companies such as Cisco, Sun, Logica and Digital Island who host the site".

News you can trust

The world renowned FT editorial is at the heart of the site, with a special focus on 14 key industries and with news updated throughout the day by the 500-strong integrated print and online global newsroom. Their concerted aim is daily to break between three and five major stories in each sector – with lots of hot links and a look at the influential people behind the news.

Michael adds, "We have a team of 120 people working on the new portal, the site's functionality has been extended to embrace share quotes, a global archive, news by email, community, personal office and business chat rooms. It's quite an incredible agenda, currently producing a massive 2.5m registered users compared to 250,000 last year," says Michael proudly. "A recent survey of users shows that 70% of users come to the site twice a week. As a further inducement we are planning a loyalty/reward scheme."

"My primary aim is for the new FT.com to become the leading Internet resource for business people everywhere, helping them to make sense of a complex, rapidly changing world."

Strengthening the links

In terms of e-commerce, FT.com has established a number of key partnerships with high profile sites such as Travelocity, Chateauonline and lastminute.com. "Selecting partners is crucial," Michael emphasises. "At the FT we only want to work with the best, to ensure our customers are getting value for money and the best possible service."

Staying ahead of the competition is crucial for the site's continued success. Michael is achieving it by continually updating the site, aggressively marketing what the site can offer business people, and above all by keeping users and encouraging loyalty through quality of content and high-profile partnerships.

Michael's top tips for those setting up an e-business are: "Be completely obsessed, do it fast and do it violently! For traditional businesses, be prepared to completely transform and do all you can to take the key strengths of the business onto the Net".

The ups and downs

Michael talks about the strengths and weaknesses of the Net. "On the positive side, the Net is transforming archaic business models and making literally tons of information available to anyone for free. News and information is now widely available for no charge and the Net has truly revolutionised business models. Negatively, the Net's drawback is its current speed and high UK access charges." Michael sees the future of the Net as changing very rapidly: "The Web is moving into digital TV and the wireless world. Soon people will be using the Net in their kitchens and their cars".

Michael's heroes

"My personal dot com hero is John Taysom, the first person to put Reuters news available on Yahoo! without charge. My favourite websites include Yahoo! because it is simple and effective; the Google search engine because it's cool and funky, and I tend to use the more obvious brands when it comes to buying online, being a regular at Amazon and, of course, using FT.com!"

The music world is Michael's main interests outside of the Net. During his time at Reuters he regularly played in a punk rock band. He also enjoys eating out, travelling and strolling by the river. Above all, devoting himself to his family – his wife and two young children.

B2B

Transforming business-to-business relationships

B2B
Transforming business-to-business relationships

B2B is a quiet revolution transforming business-to-business relationships. Although business to business trade over the Internet does not receive the media coverage of B2C, business to consumer, it is receiving huge corporate investment, alongside increasing interest from the Venture Capitalists.

Large companies can have thousands of suppliers and employees. Managing both your human resources and your procurement over the Internet are just two huge ways of reducing costs and improving productivity that the Internet delivers.

Making information accessible for employees from anywhere makes it easier for everyone to do a better job. From using the Internet/intranet to provide customer presentations and sales data to the salesforce, to sharing marketing campaigns across the world to online personnel handbooks for everyone – teamwork, productivity and collaboration are all part of the benefits of getting businesses online.

B2B saves costs, e-procurement can make double digit savings and given the amounts spent on purchasing, even down to office supplies, this is enough to generate a competitive advantage. Ford, General Motors, British Airways, are just a few of the big names who have announced e-procurement strategies. You only have to go back to good old fashioned economies to understand why this is so important – matching buyers and sellers in an open market gives near perfect conditions to reduce prices to the optimum.

The B2B heroes have taken the power of the Internet to the very heart of business. They have gone beyond customer facing websites and use the Internet to manage all or part of the supply chain. By dot com-ming their supplier and partner interactions they recognise the competitive advantage gained. The dot com-med supply chain not only reduces costs but it also improves delivery times and service levels.

Online businesses have access to more information, meaning that buyers can make more accurate decisions. It's a simple model just like giving customers better service, B2B gives buyers access to more suppliers. And it's not just big business that benefits: mondus brings buying power and economics to the small and medium, SME, market.

All the heroes interviewed for this section recognised the competitive edge an online supply chain gives, linking everyone involved in developing, manufacturing, distributing and selling products.

B2B heroes are raising productivity and improving communication across companies both internally and externally.

Many companies are changing the way they do business. With competitive pressures getting greater every day many businesses have decided to focus on what they are good at and outsource the rest.

Exodus allows companies to focus on what they are good at with the knowledge that their IT strategy is being delivered by experts at a lower cost. Companies no longer have to worry about running the technology, recruiting staff, availability, scalability and reliability – they have found a partner in service providers such as Exodus and Planet Online that do this for them.

Many of the heroes in this section provide business and Internet services that help get businesses online faster. From business incubation services to helping small businesses get online. The Internet is being used across the business value chain to dramatically improve buying processes, reduce costs of distribution, share information, and deliver a new competitive edge.

Rouzbeh Pirouz – mondus

John Beaumont – Planet Online

In a Web world skewed in favour of the consumer, it's refreshing to also find dot com business-to-business heroes. mondus and the people behind it, aren't just being successful over the Web – but are having fun whilst doing so. The site is the joint brainchild of two ex-Rhodes Scholars – German-born Alex Straub and Canadian Rouzbeh Pirouz.

Explains Rouzbeh, CEO of mondus, "mondus is all about re-engineering the business-to-business model. Basic surgery will eventually re-arrange the choreography of how small to medium-sized businesses sell to each other".

"Traditionally, the buyer and supplier relationship has been weighed down with questions, not just about product cost and quality, but order pipelines and delivery times. Businesses have also endured the hassle of locating likely buyers/suppliers in the first place, and having to deal with them by phone, fax or face-to-face meetings. By using mondus the buyer can 'cherry pick' suppliers without the need for time-consuming individual bid processes or face-to-face dealings."

Web dating for business

Once registered with mondus, buyers go online, and indicate what they want to buy. Using specially developed proprietary software, the people at mondus match requests to a database of suppliers. The requests are sent to suppliers to respond with cost, delivery times and any other information requested by the buyer. mondus then forwards replies to the buyer.

Up to 30 requests for quotes an hour can be generated and emailed to suppliers. New suppliers are continually added to the mondus database. Mondus also offers buyers and suppliers access to Dun & Bradstreet corporate and financial information, which supports the key process of selecting ideal business partners.

From text book to Web page

"Alex and I met at Oxford," recalls Rouzbeh. "While we were in New York for an annual Rhodes Scholar meeting we discovered a mutual concern for the lack of services available online for small to medium-sized businesses (SMEs). Of those that were online, services were severely restricted, so opportunities on the Net were few and far between."

"With the setting-up of mondus we focused on creating a business-to-business Web environment with tools that would make SMEs more efficient in the way they bought and sold their products and services to each other. Mondus helps both demand and supply communities expand business, knowledge and efficiency offerings."

From the start in February 1999, when Alex and Rouzbeh turned their business plan into a competition entry, their idea looked like a winner. Their entry, which beat some 1600 others, won the *Sunday Times* and 3i Technology Catapult Competition with a prize of £1m in funding to kick start mondus. Further investment followed. By late 1999 mondus was valued at $60m and became one of Europe's largest Internet start-ups.

"With the setting-up of mondus we focused on creating a business-to-business Web environment with tools that would make SMEs more efficient in the way they bought and sold their products and services to each other. mondus helps both demand and supply communities expand business, knowledge and efficiency offerings."

"In early 1999 it was just Alex and I. Now we have a global team of 110 people. We are the world's first global online business-to-business marketplace designed exclusively to meet the procurement needs of SMEs. We have operations in the UK, US, France, Germany and Sweden."

Golden rules with a Midas touch

With the company's Midas touch, what can Rouzbeh pass on to budding Web entrepreneurs looking for that crock of gold at the end of the Internet rainbow? Rouzbeh confides, "Think how Internet technology can create a website where business can be conducted at high speeds. Use that technology to change peoples' habits. Next, be courageous when looking for funding; if you have an idea, believe in it and be aggressive in getting it funded. And last – get the right people. You need people who are energetic and highly motivated".

E-commerce is Rouzbeh's answer for traditional businesses. "These businesses have been in a market reactionary mode for years – not leading by example but trying to catch up by setting up websites with an electronic commerce face. Their value to customers will reside in how innovative they are, not how easily they ape and copy others."

But large businesses should not be afraid. It only takes vision says Rouzbeh. "The Web offers tremendous potential in offering precise communication with customers. All businesses, both large and small can now talk to their customers as if they were having a one-to-one conversation."

Practising what they preach

Net-savvy analysts and commentators who have seen the future of how businesses trade predict it's going to be very much along the mondus online model – which is also a great case study for would-be dot com heroes. Apart from addressing the needs of the business-to-business community it offers a real economic lifeline for small to medium-sized businesses who may find the low costs and high efficiencies of trading over the Web the key elements that keep them in business.

One thing for certain is that thanks to Rouzbeh Pirouz and Alex Straub, any perfect business-to-business matches are no longer made in heaven but over the Web.

The Virgin Biznet portal,
providing business
management and Internet
services, is the brainchild
of Mylene Curtis CEO,
who recognised the need
for services and support
for small businesses.

mylene curtis

Net-ready entrepreneur

virginbiz.net

Finding the easier way...

In 1995, Mylene Curtis found herself with too much to do and too little time to do it. Having just had her third child and in the throes of an MBA, she thought that there must be an easier way for working mothers to buy groceries.

The prohibitively high costs of transactional websites prevented her idea becoming dot com reality, nevertheless Mylene would not be discouraged. Fervently she maintained that the primary objective of the Internet service was to further ease people's lives.

...and delivering it over the Internet

That is exactly the objective of Virgin Biznet; as created, launched and managed by Mylene. A combination of portalled virtual business management and Internet services, Virgin Biznet was set up to address the lack of services and support for small businesses. While for several years it had been obvious that eventually every business needed to get onto the Internet, until Virgin Biznet entered the market, there was no fast or affordable way for them to do so.

As Mylene herself recognised, a business required five or six suppliers to trade successfully online – not to mention a budget of many thousands of pounds. Small businesses simply did not have the time or the money. An ex-consultant and hence small business herself, Mylene not only empathised, but also took appropriate action.

Virgin Biznet specialises in providing a direct response to the requirements of small businesses. It offers every aspect needed to help them harness the Web and set it to work, from Internet access and domain name services, to merchant accounts and secure payment gateways. Businesses gain the benefit of commercial expertise, accrue a sense of community and, above all, grow and thrive.

From Net-ready to Net-enabled

Virgin Biznet's success has been one of Mylene's greatest achievements. From 'a blank sheet of paper' she created a business plan of a calibre to satisfy the Virgin Group, leading to 'standards equivalent of a top Venture Capitalist' as described by Mylene.

Unsurprisingly, Virgin vigorously protects their brand and values, which from the beginning confronted Mylene with one of the hardest sales of her career. Through sheer perseverance, Mylene achieved her goal and today Virgin Biznet enjoys a healthy growth and renowned reputation for truly understanding the challenges faced by Net-ready but not-yet-enabled small businesses.

Mylene attributes this success to a combination of factors. Firstly, Virgin Biznet offers a much-needed one-stop service at an extremely competitive cost. It helps customers to increase not only their earnings but also savings in costs and time. And it is jargon-free. Above all, her innovation achieved her original objective of helping to make people's lives easier. Virgin Biznet links with them on an emotional as well as technical level and directly addresses their business challenges. In short, Virgin Biznet adds value.

"Decide how much you want to give away and how much you want to earn. Choose whether you want to compromise your lifestyle by earning less during the early days yet retaining a bigger portion of the business."

Solve problems – offer opportunities

It comes as no surprise that Mylene's advice to new Internet companies is in keeping with her own experience. Understanding customers comes top of her list. Next, she advises, "Remove the customers' problems and offer them an opportunity." Avoiding jargon is vital too, as is the need for strategic partners. As Mylene points out: "They may be direct competitors but they can help your performance". She also advises that at an early stage the financial structure should receive close examination. "Decide how much you want to give away and how much you want to earn. Choose whether you want to compromise your lifestyle by earning less during the early days yet retaining a bigger portion of the business."

A woman's place is on the Internet

Mylene is characteristically optimistic on the future of the Internet. As a working mother, with limited leisure time, the Net has in fact improved her lifestyle. Despite a demanding job, Mylene is still able to leave the office by 6 o'clock. She can continue her professional work at any place or time. Indeed, eToys has replaced Father Christmas.

Mylene recognises the potential of the Internet as a business environment for women. Women start forty percent of small businesses. She claims that the Net delivers a combination of accessibility and flexibility to working mothers which is why she maintains that the dot com start-ups of the future will, in the main, be spearheaded by women.

Ask her to be specific on her initial opportunities and Mylene shows how she earned her reputation as a first-to-market dot com hero. "Keep looking for the gaps and jumping in." Considering that's how Virgin Biznet started, you can be sure that Mylene will maintain one step ahead, identifying needs and delivering answers.

Larry Levy, founder of the Protégé incubation service, has the enviable task of making millionaires of technology entrepreneurs. Yet despite his success, Larry has a strong sense of social responsibility and dreams of Internet access for all.

larry levy

Dream maker

protégé.co.uk

Protégé investor in the future

Larry Levy has a unique perspective and inside knowledge of the future of the Internet. His company, Protégé, provides an incubation service to turn Internet entrepreneurs into millionaires. So when Larry Levy talks about his vision of the Net, its opportunities and potential pitfalls, he's not guessing, he knows. By providing investment in exchange for equity, Protégé is a hothouse for new talent and the starting point for many of the services and technologies we'll take for granted tomorrow.

Larry has always been ahead of his time. While running the European arm of Delrina in 1994, he was involved in the invention of CyberJack, an early browser. Soon after he considered starting his own portal, but no ISP could offer pan-European support at the time.

Yet with Protégé, Larry has the opportunity to see today's vision become tomorrow's products and services. The largest, most well-established and respected European Econet, Protégé has built 24 European businesses creating five millionaires in just four years.

Be first, be focused, be flexible

Larry is happy to pass on his tips for would-be technology leaders. Being first to market provides an immeasurable advantage. Focus too is critical. But, having the flexibility to react to changing circumstances is just as important. As Larry says, "Young founders often stick to their guns too long".

Nevertheless, as Larry emphasises, you can't run an Internet business by the same rules as an ordinary business. The 'Internet rhythm' is totally new and traditional business dynamics don't work. He believes that possibly the most difficult decision an entrepreneur has to make is the selection of the right equity partner. Larry believes that "In the apparent gold rush of Internet funding and start-up launches, the entrepreneur must keep front of mind his or her own questions to a potential equity partner. These should always include: what do they offer other than money?"

Larry predicts the creation of a whole new Internet dimension, with its own standards and regulations. Yet, he worries that this will lead to a dual society of information-haves and have-nots. This may well be addressed by the next generation of access devices, such as interactive TV, but it's an issue that Protégé is currently addressing. Larry is determined that "from a social perspective, we should ensure that everyone will have access".

The rise of wireless communications, device agnosticism, productivity applications to help people manage their lives, these are the future of the Internet according to Larry Levy.

But he doesn't just talk about them. You can be sure that at Protégé, they are already well on their way to becoming reality.

For John Beaumont, Managing Director of Planet Online, which provides operational, technical and management support for Freeserve, there are no barriers. A unique combination of visionary and action man, he can see the potential of the Web but he isn't dazzled by it.

When did you first get involved in the Net?
1998 – Energis' acquisition of Planet.

What is the company's greatest achievement?
Planet's operational and technical support for Freeserve's explosive growth development.

Key behind site
Vision and quality people for implementation.

How is it unique?
Customer focused, leading edge with a 'can do' action attitude.

What are your three top tips for building an Internet business?
Vision, Management Focus, Opportunism.

How did you secure finances?
A subsidiary of an FTSE 100 company.

Golden opportunities
Audio/video streaming; e-commerce.

How will you stay ahead?
Listening to customers and looking to exploit technology advances.

Any Net predictions?
It will become more pervasive but it is not a panacea.

Favourite sites
Yahoo!, Freeserve, Charles Schwab, Pointcast.

Greatest thing about the Net
It's available anytime nearly anywhere.

Worst thing
It's available anytime nearly anywhere – but we should not forget more traditional ways of people communicating.

john beaumont

Available anytime

theplanet.net

Any advice for other start-ups?
Have the vision but focus on the day-to-day, even hour-by-hour, to ensure customer satisfaction and loyalty.

Advice for a traditional business
Think radically about new business models.

Your vision of the Web's future
The network of the new millennium.

What inspires you?
There are no barriers – 'impossible' does not exist.

What should inspire others?
The opportunities to create sustainable businesses and wealth, as well as have fun.

Other interests
Good company, good food and good wine; travel; watching sport; reading fiction.

Mark Suster, CEO of
Build Online, brings
together the architect,
constructor and
materials suppliers
online to reduce time
and costs surrounding
building projects.

mark suster

Online constructor
build-online.com

"Understand the customer." That's the prime piece of advice from Mark Suster. He should know since Mark is the CEO of build-online.com – a rapidly growing business-to-business Internet enterprise that's creating community within the tough and unforgiving world of building and construction, said to be worth £520bn in Europe alone.

Launched formally in 1999, Build Online brings together the architect, constructor and materials suppliers to reduce time and costs surrounding building projects. Put simply, it enables better planning in the ordering of materials and services. Through doing so, the construction company and building sites don't receive materials like steel, bricks or glazing before they're required. This avoids building sites turning into vast warehouses for idle materials and helps reduce their attractiveness to professional thieves. Costs for the materials manufacturer and distributor are greatly reduced since they only need to make and deliver products when they are actually required.

Better built – all round

Says Mark, "Build Online uses the Internet to secure benefits from IT for the building industry. By using techniques like EDI we're helping both large and small companies gain cost savings and efficiencies which they would have only dreamed about a few years ago.

"Unlike other websites servicing the construction industry, Build Online is not a portal. We're creating relationships between major players in design and construction. In this way Build Online becomes a project manager, driving through benefits to all. All that's required is a PC and a browser to access our services. Build Online's membership is free and provides access for news, information and email services."

Reducing costs – elevating expectations

Build Online estimates that e-construction can deliver 23% savings in European construction and reduce construction project completion times by 15%. That amounts to annual industry savings of over £119bn.

Back to basics

Clearly Build Online is an all-round winner. But how did the idea for the company first emerge?

In 1997 Build Online's founder and president Brian Moran, along with a 'business angel', injected some basic but crucial start-up capital to get the idea off the drawing board. It provided 'proof of concept' and indicated to Brian that he had a winning idea. In the following year, he linked up with Mark and set out to build up the idea to a fully fleshed-out 'dot com' – a brilliant business plan secured £2m worth of funding. By August 1999 build-online.com became such an attractive proposition that additional Venture Capital investment to the tune of £16.5m flowed in.

The story according to Mark

Californian by birth, and an unashamed technologist, Mark enjoyed early successes whilst working for Andersen Consulting in San Francisco and Los Angeles. He introduced local and wide area networking to both West Coast locations. For the first time, employees could communicate electronically with their clients. EDI helped speed up transfer of documentation and information between clients and consultants. By the late Nineties, he set about identifying and fixing BT's Internet strategy.

"I met Brian in Chicago in 1998," says Mark, "and was very impressed with the Build Online concept. It had obvious benefits to the construction industry from day one. Over the past few months we've seen the influence of Build Online in the way companies in the industry have fundamentally changed working practices inside their own organisations, for instance, picking up on EDI and supply chain management techniques.

"I believe that business to business is where the Net is going to make a far more important and fundamental contribution to global economies than business to consumer Web initiatives. I'm sure there will be massive consolidation as investors start asking some crucial questions."

Success that sets in as quickly as cement
Build Online is currently managing projects to the value of £125m. This includes major redevelopment work for the Irish government in Dublin. Like many of Build Online's customers, they've benefited from Build's simplified procurement process, speedy access to an improved roster of suppliers, enhanced management, control, auditing and archiving of projects.

Build Online's UK operation has rapidly grown from just four people early in 1999 to 60 by early 2000. Continental European operations are also set to grow, with new locations just established in Paris and Dusseldorf.

Advice to wannabes
Mark advises future dot com heroes to "Understand your value proposition and existing industry structure. Appreciate in advance what your entry into the market will achieve, since that's when you'll create your friends and your enemies. And develop a world class product!"

"Next, get a seasoned management team in place as early as possible – the need for good people is paramount. Seek external finance and don't be afraid to ask for the right level of investment since that's key in securing the success of the business. And make everyone an owner in the company. Finally, focus on execution. Grand strategies are out. Execution is king. Make fast decisions but don't get hung up on making wrong decisions."

As for the future, Mark comments, "I'm convinced the Net is going to be a significant factor in job creation and wealth creation. I've already seen it with Build Online – not only have we created jobs in our own company but we've seen it in the construction industry too. The new economy is producing a democratic revolution in that it enables bright people, who would otherwise be lost deep inside organisations, to be dynamic, show their abilities and make a difference to those companies."

Mark is totally engrossed in Build Online and happy for it. "The work is demanding, but no-one said it would be easy. Sleep has become the enemy. I'm keen to grow the business but while I'm sure the people around me will say I'm focused and assertive, I hope they will also say I'm fair."

Sounds like the perfect foundations to build a sprawling Web-business.

"The new economy is producing a democratic revolution in that it enables bright people, who would otherwise be lost deep inside organisations, to be dynamic, show their abilities and make a difference to those companies."

Forced into the Internet
kicking and screaming,
Julia Groves, Launch
Director, soon became
addicted and is now
passionate. eVentures
partners with the most
successful US companies
wanting to launch their
brands in the UK.

julia groves

E-matchmaker

eventures.co.uk

When did you first get involved in the Net?

In March 1995. I was forced into it kicking and screaming – being the youngest in the Marketing Communications department at British Airways, I had little choice. Got a taste for it within about three months when I realised it was as much about marketing as technology, and that there were no silver haired 50 year olds who had done it all before. I've been addicted since about August 1997.

What is your greatest achievement?

I think the little achievements in the early days were the most important because they helped build faith in the organisation that this was really happening.

Key behind your business?

Speed to market and finding and growing the talent to deliver market leading customer propositions in the UK.

What are your three top tips for building an Internet business?

People, Pace, Passion.

How did you secure finances?

eVentures is a 50:50 joint venture between Softbank and ePartners – an Internet Venture Capitalist backed by News Corp.

Any advice for other start-ups?

Don't compromise on your talent.

Advice for a traditional business

Get humble, get nimble, act as if you're about to go out of business, cannibalise.

Your vision of the Web's future

Invisible, constant, wireless – saving me time on the dull stuff so I can spend more time on the good stuff in life.

Golden opportunities

Reward shared more equitably between the talent and the organisation, the rise of the individual!

How will you stay ahead?

Take the risks, make the mistakes, grab the learning and share it as broadly as possible.

Any Net predictions?

Wouldn't dare...

Personal hero

Always my boss.

Favourite sites

tesco.co.uk, investor.com, thestandard.com, gatherround.com... mostly practical stuff.

Greatest thing about the Net

The power of knowledge for the customer.

Worst thing

It doesn't quite work yet.

What inspires you?

That cartoon that said 'Daddy, what did you do in the Internet Wars?'

What should inspire others?

People believing in them.

Soundbite

I'm not sure about a soundbite, but my philosophy is 'Bigger Harder Faster More!'

Other interests

Most things I can't afford, most things I shouldn't touch, very little that is good for me and some fabulous friends and family that gave me the confidence to do it all.

> "Get humble, get nimble, act as if you're about to go out of business, cannibalise."

As one of the first people to realise the potential of Application Service Provision, Paul Barry-Walsh has also been one of the first to reap the benefits, as founder of NetStore, the UK's leading provider of managed solutions over the Web.

paul barry-walsh

Founder and solution provider

netstore.com

Paul Barry-Walsh's uncanny ability to discriminate between dot com fads and business trends secures his position as a dot com leader's leader. In 1986 he formed Safetynet Plc the world's first dedicated computer disaster recovery company. It maintained a compound year on year growth of 30%.

Ten years later, Paul launched NetStore, the world's leading provider of managed solutions for the distributed enterprise. Essentially, NetStore is an Applications Service Provider. It provides the latest business software applications available to companies to download via the Web as and wherever they need them. NetStore's service harnesses the Internet's global roaming abilities, allowing everyone from a salesperson on the road, to a Vice President behind a desk, to access documents, files and applications securely and without fear of an in-house system being unable to cope.

Simple ingenuity

When Paul first conceived NetStore, he sought an intelligent method to securely back-up laptops and PCs. He discovered appropriate Internet enabled technology in Boston. Paul negotiated the distributions rights to use it in the UK and then set about to raise the necessary corporate finance.

Paul was used to working in Internet time – so-called 'dog years' (seven Web years equates to one normal year). "We wanted to get online quickly, so invested a couple of hundred of thousands of pounds to get the company going. Things have really taken off. Apart from starting SafetyNet and working with partners like Reuters, this has been one of my greatest achievements to date."

The only certainty on the Web is change

"Over the years our business model has evolved. Every Web start-up must be flexible enough to change their business model. In our case we're positioned as an Applications Services Provider. This is currently one of the hottest of the hot commodities on the Web. Companies can concentrate on their core competencies, scale requirements and know the cost of application software usage in advance. Just as companies don't generate their own electrical power or run their own water systems – both commodities – so they can now buy as much or as little business software applications as they need. For example, their ideal measure of Microsoft Exchange or Oracle – scalable at affordable monthly fees. It gives the kind of power and flexibility normally unavailable to small to middle size companies."

How hot is hot?

According to Paul, whilst the hype about the Internet is cooling, the ASP business is getting more heated. "Just as everyone is familiar with ISPs, soon everybody will be raving about ASPs. At one NetStore conference alone there was standing room only. "It cost us £100,000 to put the conference on. We raised £98,000 in sponsorship through companies like BT, Microsoft, Cisco and Oracle who keenly wanted to be associated with ASPs." (NetStore secured the first European contract to provide Microsoft Exchange via an ASP facility.)

Well funded – well founded

Paul acknowledges that many great people have brilliant Web ideas. He recommends they get their enterprises properly funded. A year after NetStore's initial funding and 3i's investment of £900,000 in 1997, the company announced further financing to fund future growth. The investment totals an additional £3m and is split between the Venture Capital arms of NatWest and Barclays Banks and 3i.

Marketing rules

According to Paul, enduring dot com heroes will not necessarily be those with just the best technology. "They need to stake space for themselves – that requires clever marketing. The Web is applicable for any kind of business wishing to reach the market quickly and efficiently. Marketing helps you get the right ideas." He recommends that e-entrepreneurs should lift a page out the American book of e-business success stories. "Get the hype, get it out there and have the site ready quickly."

Paul's next tip, "If the site is going to be your shop-front, be sure that it's available constantly. It's not like running a chain of 500 high street stores. If one closes – there are 499 still open. On the Web, downtime adds up to share devaluation. That's why I am also involved with another company called E-Continuity which ensures sites are always available. If you are an established traditional business and not already on the Web start feeling nervous because your competitors are going straight to the market".

Keeping Mum

Paul believes that sites featuring complicated functionality are unattractive to surfers. "Go for the mother who has only ever been on the Web once. Make the whole experience incredibly easy. Eventually surfers will be able to talk to Web sites, that's when the Web's simplicity will attract a universal acceptance.

Paul's heroes and zeroes

"My personal dot com hero is Tim Koogle. He was the CEO of Yahoo! He set up a whole bunch of smart deals. It's not difficult to raise money in the current environment. It is difficult however to raise money and make a profit. Yahoo! has a pretty bright future.

"In terms of great sites, I love the Telegraph. You can flick through histories of stories. It is very well constructed. The greatest thing about the Net is that it is an amazing information source; everything from diagnosing an ailment to someone who bought a Gulf Stream Four aircraft via it. The worst thing is when sites go down or are not properly built, or everything stops and you don't know why. It's frustrating.

"Mind you I am inspired by the opportunities that the Web opens up. Take telephone banking. It came in ten years ago – some hundred years after the telephone was invented. We haven't even begun to conceive what the Web can do in the decade, let alone the next century."

Whatever happens, you can be sure that Paul will be one of the first to take advantage of the trend by delivering just what the market needs.

> "If the site is going to be your shop-front, be sure that it's available constantly. It's not like running a chain of 500 high street stores. If one closes – there are 499 still open. On the Web, downtime adds up to share devaluation."

Kim Polese, CEO and Co-founder of Marimba, an Internet infrastructure company providing services management, measures her success by that of her customers. Quality of service, especially in terms of delivery, is critical and execution is her driving force.

kim polese

Internet service manager

marimba.com

Kim Polese, the CEO and Co-founder of Marimba Inc. is a woman of worth. Her company went public in 1999. Marimba's primary product, Castanet, allows corporations to deliver efficiently software and information across the Web. It has commanded a leading position in the market. Marimba boasts over 100 customers, including major contracts from Bear, Stearns & Co.; Charles Schwab & Co.; The Home Depot; and Sears Roebuck & Co.

So what makes one of the most successful people in Silicon Valley tick?

"I was a product manager and Arthur and Sami were senior engineers on the Java project. Jonathan Payne had also been on the project, but he had gone up to Starwave Corp. I remember being on the phone once with him. We were saying, 'We ought to launch a company.' It started the wheels turning in the back of my mind."

"Before long the four of us got together at a bar at the World Wide Web Consortium in Boston in December '95. We decided to prove we could start a company. 'Let's write a mock business plan, figure out what the product would be and what the market would be and how we would price it and how we would sell it. Let's do all of that before we even go off and start the company.' Between Christmas and New Year, we met every day, eight hours a day, at a café or over at Arthur's home and we created this business plan."

"Arthur, Sami and Jonathan built a great product. They are three of the most brilliant engineers that I've encountered in my career. Arthur is someone people look to as a visionary, and he also has a great business sense. Then in the autumn of 1996, Steve Williams left Tivoli and joined us as vice president of sales."

Some analysts and press have suggested Marimba was valued as an Internet company, but really is not. What do you think about that?

"We're not an "Internet.com," but then neither are we an enterprise software company. We're an Internet infrastructure company, which is the crossroads of the two. What we do we call ISM, or Internet Services Management. We're managing the delivery of ongoing services."

What do you think of the rising application service provider business?

"When we started the company, we envisioned a world in which applications would be rented. Software Providers thought we were a little nutty. But our technology was designed for exactly that. Documents and applications will ultimately be sold as services over the Net, and we can sell Castanet to the ASP."

Is there anything wrong with the term Push Technology?

"Yeah, the P word. Back in late 1996, when we first released our product to the market, there wasn't an existing market category that we could easily fit into. We weren't an electronic software delivery [ESD] company. We weren't a network systems management company like Tivoli Systems Inc. or Computer Associates International Inc.

"We're not an 'Internet.com' but then neither are we an enterprise software company. We're an Internet infrastructure company, which is the crossroads of the two. What we do we call ISM, or Internet Services Management. We're managing the delivery of ongoing services."

"The only category that seemed to be remotely related was this new novelty called push. That essentially got assigned to us by the market. Anytime you introduce a new product a little ahead of the curve, the market will find a place to put you. So push was it."

What is your company philosophy?

"The company values execution – delivery, reality, making customers successful from day one – over hype, concept and ego. It's about exceeding expectations, especially making customers successful.

"As CEO, I have much faith in having regular brainstorming sessions. We have these at least once a month. We get in the room and remain for a half or full day with a white board. We force ourselves to think about what has been happening around us in the market over the last month. What are we hearing and learning from customers? What improvements can we make? Where do we need to be six months from now? This industry is changing so fast, you have to be extremely vigilant."

"We have all-hands meetings in the company at which I bring everyone up-to-date on what we're planning during the month. We have 'lunch with Kim'. Anyone can sign up, go out to lunch. Internal communication is critical for this fast-moving industry."

Did you change the business model as time went on?

"We evolved the business model to address what customers were asking for. We initially focused on the Global 1000 companies, like Ford Motor Co. and Chrysler Corp. and Schwab."

When you first launched your company a lot of press said "There is nothing to Marimba except a very attractive female CEO". Do you think that was essentially a sexist presentation of what was happening with your company?

"My reaction was not concern about sexism, but disappointment on behalf of my company, my Co-founders and our customers. Everyone in our company was working really hard to build a great company, and everyone knew we have a fabulous product that works wonders. It was a disservice to Marimba and to our customers. It was a reaction to the oddity and the novelty of a woman CEO. But it didn't really bother me at the end of the day because I knew we were going to be successful, and I knew we were going to kick butt."

Exodus takes care of the important matters of the Internet like hosting, bandwidth and security, leaving their customers to concentrate on their core business. Ellen Hancock is the CEO and outsourcing visionary.

Talk to any Venture Capitalist and there are a number of givens if you're ever going to attract investment and become a successful dot com. As well as the 'idea' itself, of course, you need good people, a knock-out website, great marketing and robust IT plumbing. That's where Exodus Communications kicks in. For over five years Exodus has pioneered the Internet data centre market, climbing in the process in 1999 from 76 to 11 in Business Week's Information Technology 100.

The company's forte is provision of complex Internet hosting architectures for dot coms and enterprises in mission critical operations, Exodus offers sophisticated system and network management solutions, along with technology services that deliver ace performances for customers' websites. Additional services cover website performance monitoring and measurement.

But it wasn't always like that. Back when it started in 1994, Exodus was actually an Internet Service Provider – an ISP when ISPs were a very rare breed of IT animal. Explains Ellen M. Hancock, CEO of Exodus, "Exodus was more of an ISP which is why it's exodus.net. Then it moved into the hosting business and I believe we are currently positioned well in terms of Web hosting, the leader in the US and our vision is to be leader in Europe and Asia. In fact, we've moved from being a hosting company to one that's now really focused on complex Web hosting."

The company's business model changed about the time of Ellen's arrival at Exodus – March 1998 – following 32 years with IBM where she rose to become Senior Vice President and Group Executive in charge of the Network Hardware Division before moving to first National Semiconductor, then Apple.

ellen hancock

The master outsourcer

exodus.net

Since 1998 Exodus has gained a whole new reputation amongst the growing legion of dot coms, as well as IT technologists, as the supplier of superior value-added services. Ellen comments, "It's the amount of value-added services that the customers look to you to provide and, for example, the ability to work with them on very large websites, and the ability to work with them on security.

We got very much involved in the recent denial of service attacks and we worked with our customers on tape backup, disk backup and caching."

In the mid-nineties, the Exodus promise was just that but it wasn't too long before some early pioneering Internet start-ups backed Exodus including the likes of yahoo.com, lycos.com and ebay.com who all took the plunge and backed the company. Today, Exodus has the dominant share of the Web hosting market – some 30% of the world's top websites and estimates the Web hosting market to grow exponentially by some 76% per year.

Exodus estimates that $43bn in e-commerce business alone was done over its hosting servers in 1998. Says Ellen, "In 1998 a lot of outsourcing was in fact being done by the dot coms but several of us in the industry indicated, as we went into1999, we would see the enterprise moving to the Internet and we clearly have seen that. Right now 49% of our customer base are enterprises and they're coming in with very large websites. We do believe the Application Service Provider market will continue to grow and we currently provide a lot of the infrastructure for the ASP market.

"We see the continued rollout of bandwidth as an opportunity, whether it's DSL to the home or whether it's wireless. And we do believe these are important. We've already watched a lot of the websites going from doing some e-commerce to sites that do a lot of e-commerce and we're seeing an increased usage of security, backup and restore capabilities. I think we're seeing a maturity in the Internet but, having said that, we believe we're in the very early stages of network technology and there's a lot of invention left for us to make it as robust as some earlier technologies we've seen."

Exodus is a 'pure play' in that it only hosts websites and maintains clear focus on its core competency around the world where it has, today, 20 data centres in fulltime operation. There are sixteen in the States and three outside; in London, Tokyo and a brand new one in Frankfurt, with another fourteen planned for completion during 2000. Outsourcing on this scale for large corporates – and fresh-faced start-ups – is obviously attractive since it frees up the customer to focus on their business while Exodus takes care of important matters like hosting, bandwidth and security behind the scenes.

"We don't hire the customers' employees. They have the ability to continue to work on their own websites while we make sure the sites are functioning correctly, and that they're being monitored. We review the performance and we just acquired a performance monitoring company," explains Ellen.

The growing use of video and audio streaming in both Net-based business and consumer fields is being addressed by Exodus's newly acquired equity interest in Mirror Image Internet Enterprise, which will boost the company's content and delivery distribution capability on a global scale. Here Mirror Image's worldwide network of content access points will handle higher Internet traffic volumes at far greater speeds for Exodus's customers. That's all part of Exodus's mission to track closely the evolvement of the Internet.

"We're working very closely with DSL providers to understand the impact of DSL," comments Ellen, "so when the industry follows through on some more enhanced network technologies we would be very supportive of that. We watch what the changes are but do not lose our main focus."

So, who are Ellen's heroes and what advice can she offer either start-up or major corporates? One hero is Margaret Thatcher. Says Ellen, "I would say that I was impressed by women who accomplished things like Margaret Thatcher and I'm impressed with people in technology areas like Jack Hayward who was vice chairman of IBM and a mentor of mine. I've got quite a few heroes in the industry."

And advice? The word is Partnerships. Explains Ellen, "I would say that taking money just for the sake of making an announcement that you've got money is not something that's overly important. Much more important is the strength of the relationship and whether the partner really is there for you and whether for them it was a simple financial transaction.

"We had a panel discussion with some of our customers recently and the panel moderator asked questions about what was really important to start-ups. Was it funding? Was it partnerships? Was it first to market? We all said – getting money is not the important part. Strength of partnerships and relationships are more important than just the dollars."

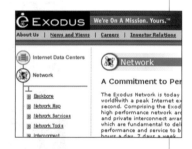

wider web & new interpreters

Creativity on the world's online stage

Wider Web &
New Interpreters
Creativity on the world's online stage

The Internet is the one industry that does not have a stereotypical mould. Since its conception, culture, arts, business and education have all converged. In fact, some of the people interviewed for this section of the book were surprised to be asked at all.

Yet these people, from the arts to sport industries, use the Internet to their advantage as well as any tycoon or technical whiz kid. They are the ones who have identified opportunities with a unique spin and creativity.

These are the people that keep hold of Tim Berners-Lee's vision that the Internet is for everyone. They take the power of the Internet and use it to change lives. Julie Howell of 'Jooly's Joint' has created a proactive environment full of hope for over 10,000 multiple sclerosis sufferers.

Take Pete Goss, international yachtsman and acclaimed adventurer. A decorated hero in the real world, after his dramatic rescue of French sailor Raphael Dinelli, Pete has a record of competitive excellence that includes four transatlantic and two round-the-world races. Resourceful and dynamic, Pete has always put whatever is to hand to work for him. That includes the Internet. No Luddite when it comes to technology and unafraid of uncharted waters, Pete has integrated the Internet into almost every facet of his work, from e-commerce to on-board communications. In fact, thanks to the Internet, everywhere Pete goes, we can follow.

Then there are the heroes who have genuinely added value to the Internet. With Beenz, Phil Letts has not only given the Web its own currency but transformed the concept of e-commerce incentivisation and hence marketing, as a result. In Phil's own words, "For the first time the Net has a dynamic marketing tool totally unmatched by any other Web reward scheme". As with Pete Goss, Phil's success has depended, not just on good ideas, but on being in the right place at the right time.

Yet, while these heroes embrace the Internet enthusiastically, they don't do so unconditionally. While Pete Goss wouldn't tolerate the extra weight of dot com technology on his boat if it slowed him down, film-maker Terry Gilliam, also profiled on the forthcoming pages, is a prime example of someone who recognises the darker side of the Internet. His nightmarish vision of an increasingly sanitised and domesticated Internet, dominated by the corporates, strikes a warning note.

Yet he, like many of the maverick heroes in this book, sees the Internet as a world of opportunity, in which the little guy, at least for the time being, can compete on an equal footing with the corporates. New media technology makes it possible for young film-makers to create, publish and distribute their work with a minimum of resources and backing and enjoy the freedom of their own imaginations with relative impunity.

What these heroes enjoy, above all else, is a unique vision of the Internet. Neither dazzled by its technology nor blinded by its possibilities, these are the people who have put the Web to work for them. And in the process, they have created new models.

David Bowie has revolutionised the music industry and has added an extra dimension to media, bringing a much-needed sense of personality to what could otherwise be a faceless corporate venture.

More than technology, the Internet needs people with creative personalities. These are the men and women who will be there and, by doing so, make the Web a more interesting place.

Julie Howell – Jooly's Joint

Phil Letts – Beenz

The competitive, fast-moving world of motorsport is one in which Ron Dennis, Chairman and CEO of West McLaren Mercedes, feels perfectly at home and whose values he has successfully translated to mclaren.net, the website for motorsport lovers.

When did you first get involved in the Net?

We launched the official McLaren website in 1996. So that was the start, but my children keep me up to speed with all the most exciting sites.

What is your greatest achievement?

The greatest achievement for our website has been to make the McLaren organisation more accessible to motorsport enthusiasts via our website and to provide them with an opportunity to get closer to the West McLaren Mercedes team.

Key behind site

A commitment to providing the most effective and informative website for McLaren and motorsport enthusiasts.

What are your three top tips for building an Internet business?

1. Know your audience/clients.
2. Ensure your website is easy to use and information simple to find.
3. Monitor competition.

How did you secure finances?

McLaren finances its own website and employs an external Internet company to manage the technicalities of its operation.

Any advice for other start-ups?

Consider how you can most effectively involve the Internet as part of your overall business strategy.

Advice for a traditional business

Do not neglect the Internet – it is not a leap of faith, but a vital business consideration.

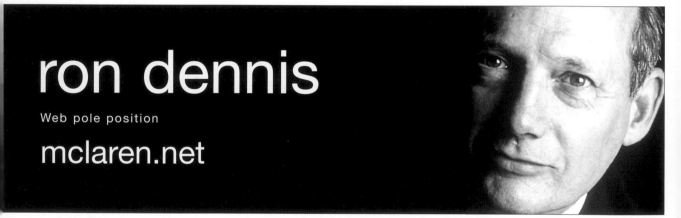

ron dennis

Web pole position

mclaren.net

How is it unique?

It is an almost exclusive source for people who wish to purchase official McLaren clothing and accessories.

Your vision of the Web's future

That the Internet will play a pivotal role in the lives of every 21st-century family and organisation.

Golden opportunities

E-commerce clearly provides a dynamic opportunity for businesses on a global basis. In terms of public relations, the Internet is also a perfect platform for establishing a rapport with visitors to your website and providing worldwide exposure for your brand image and brand values.

How will you stay ahead?

By striving to be the best.

Any Net predictions?

The Internet has developed at such an incredible pace and its scope for further evolution is almost limitless. Just a few years ago, most people were not even aware of the Internet's existence. I think it is inevitable that the Internet will continue to revolutionise the ways in which both commerce and industry operate.

Personal hero

Too many to mention.

Favourite sites

I have no specific favourite sites, but the types that appeal to me are clean, well presented, and intuitively simple to use.

Greatest thing about the Net

Organisations are able to deliver their message to a potential 160 million global Internet users – 24 hours a day, seven days a week, 52 weeks a year. No other publishing format can offer such an expansive audience.

Worst thing

There is always a delicate balance between developing a technologically advanced website and alienating Internet users with computers lacking the required upgrades.

What inspires you?

Perfection.

What should inspire others?

To understand and exploit their full potential.

Soundbite

Silence – "thought".

Any quirks or interesting facts?

Nothing I could possibly divulge!

Other interests

My family and Formula One.

"Do not neglect the Internet – it is not a leap of faith, but a vital business consideration."

International yachtsman Pete Goss is an adventurer on the Web as well as the oceans of the world. Through it he has found new sponsors, created new revenue streams, generated business leads and promoted his next major adventure.

pete goss

Web adventurer

teamphilips.com

International yachtsman Pete Goss is not into heroes. At least not the glorified and lionised media stars. He prefers the heroes who reside inside us all. The heroic act that either shows itself dramatically when the occasion or incident requires, or quietly as in a charitable role or some small way that won't make the headlines but is no less as important or as effective.

Pete is neither showy, noisy, aggressive nor egocentric. Instead he is constrained, controlled and very British – especially when it comes to his view of the major challenge that burns bright inside his head and that of his colleagues and supporters.

Setting sail for destiny

Team Philips is a massive catamaran, 120 feet long, 70 feet wide and 130 feet tall. Even with the recent setbacks, Pete plans to be at its helm when he races around the world during 2001. At £2.4m, the Team Philips vessel represents the latest in yacht racing technology. Its twin wave-piercing hulls carry the craft at speeds of up to 40 knots. The craft's construction is only half the story. On December 31st 2000 Team Philips aim to join other impressive craft to set sail from Barcelona, Spain in 'The Race', a no holds barred race around the globe featuring the largest, fastest, most sophisticated yachts ever.

Pete has always longed for adventure. Some of his greatest influences came when he was a young boy. At the time his father, a tropical agricultural consultant, took the family all over the world to virtually every continent. It was all very 'Swallows and Amazons' but it seeded in the young Pete the desire for adventure, travel and excitement.

Not surprisingly, Pete realised many of his ambitions through sailing. Today he is one of the world's most acclaimed yachtsmen, with a record of competitive excellence that includes four transatlantic and two round-the-world races.

Pete is keen to make the distinction that Team Philips and The Race are just the latest chapters in his unfolding adventure. "I'm an adventurer, not a sailor. When I was young I was fascinated by test pilots and astronauts: people with a 'true to themselves' attitude. It doesn't just have to be about climbing Mount Everest. It's often the small things that release the hero inside us."

Turning back can sometimes be the best way forward

It was no small feat when a few years ago Pete rescued Frenchman Raphael Dinelli from certain death in the Southern Ocean. Pete was taking part in the Vendee Globe non-stop single-handed race. By rescuing Dinelli, he lost a leading position in the race. "What else could I do? I received a distress message on my satellite receiver so I went back to rescue him from a storm."

Back in the calmer waters of the West Country, Pete and the Team Philips project are completing construction and fitting out of the vessel in the Totnes boatyard that has become something of a Mecca for everyone and anyone interested in and concerned with Britain's standing in oceanic racing.

"I'm an adventurer, not a sailor. When I was young I was fascinated by test pilots and astronauts: people with a 'true to themselves' attitude. It doesn't just have to be about climbing Mount Everest. It's often the small things that release the hero inside us."

Navigating the Web

Equally important for Team Philips is their website. Originally petegoss.com, a very embryonic and tentative project, the content migrated to teamphilips.com. "We've come a long way since those early days talking to Sun about their support for both the site and visitor centre. Now, we've got Sun, Musto, BT and, of course, Philips as our major sponsors.

"Not surprisingly, we've got big plans for the website. A 'must' will be regular daily reports from the boat. That includes telemetry type data in real time providing our position, speed and progress. Using our BT maritime satellite link, we also plan interviews with the crew beamed back live to the website and visitor centre."

Reaching out – anywhere

"I've learnt a lot about the Web over the past few years and have been absolutely amazed at how easily it turns communications into a two-way street – anywhere, anytime. E-commerce has not only allowed us to sell over the Web and create a new revenue stream but also helped find one of our sponsors, and that's apart from business leads, corporate hospitality and so forth that have spun off from our Web presence."

"Up to the end of 1999 our site attracted one and a half million hits a month and growing, with 76% of all visitors to site coming from overseas. We have a great level of interactivity on the site. In fact we have gone out of our way to be very inclusive with Net music, competitions, education projects and even have the involvement of the Royal Marine Band. I am sure the website visitor figure will really ramp up as soon as we start trials and get closer to the race."

And after 'The Race'? Well, of course, there are plans for books and TV documentaries but being the 'I'm a sailor not a hero' Pete is already planning his next big adventure, one that will, like the Team Philips catamaran, harness the latest in technology along with other advancements.

"I can't say too much just yet but I have no intention of taking a back seat in my life. I shall always continue to look for the challenges in life – and the hero inside others."

Sandy Nairne, Tate
Gallery's charismatic
Director of Services,
talks about how and
why he's taken
art online.

sandy nairne

Creative netrepreneur

tate.org.uk

The Tate group of galleries epitomises why the UK leads the world in the Arts. The Tate houses the national collections of British art and of international modern art from the 16th century to the present day. The original Tate Gallery on Millbank and now Tate Britain, will house work up to the end of the 19th century while Tate Modern will show the Tate's collection of 20th century art. Famed for its collection of Turners, Tate Britain also boasts works from other British artists such as Hogarth, Gainsborough, Reynolds and Constable. Tate Modern on the other hand will house work by Hockney, Bacon, Dali, Matisse, and Picasso. In Liverpool the newly opened Tate is the official North of England home for the Tate's modern works of art, while 300-plus miles south-west of Millbank is Tate St Ives, which offers a unique introduction to modern art where many works can be viewed in surroundings that inspired them.

From canvas to screen prints

The Tate has spread its flourishing success onto the Web. In the last calendar year, the site attracted an incredible 66 million hits. Currently, each day it's receiving around quarter of a million hits. Leading the Tate Gallery online team is the charismatic Sandy Nairne. He picks up the story.

"In 1998, when we originally launched our website, we avoided putting up opening times and the sort of information you'd get from hundreds of other sites. Instead we aimed to create an online database, which captured all our retained works of art." With much hard work, and even greater team effort, Sandy eventually catalogued around 25,000 pieces, 8,000 of them accompanied by illustrations.

Sandy explains the site's integral design philosophy: "We could have launched in 1996. But held off to develop a proper strategy for both the website and our public face. Wolff Olins, the design consultancy, refined the new Tate graphic identity, which you can see expressed in posters, brochures, literature, and advertising. The London design agency Nykris Digital Design applied cool simplicity throughout all aspects of the Tate website."

From May 2000 Sandy added 500 new images to the website each week. At his present rate of progress, by the end of 2001 the entire Tate collection of 50,000 images should be online. Works can be searched via a variety of methods, including an A-Z of artists. For academics, the site also provides a Library, Archive and Study Room.

Why build a new wing when you could construct another page?

A recent feature on the website called Tate Connection shows surfers how the Tate relates to other organisations in the UK and abroad. It currently includes sections on the new Partnerships Scheme, launched early in 2000 with the support of the Heritage Lottery Fund, a touring Exhibition which covers Tate Collections exhibitions and loan exhibitions made in partnership with other museums and galleries. It also features 'Links' which create the bridge to wider information sources through the 24-Hour Museum project and the BBC History Project.

Ingredients for success

Sandy is clear about his intentions for the site. "The website must achieve three things. First, explain our strategy behind various locations, from Tate Britain through to Tate St Ives. Second, to be a repository for as much information as we could provide on all our collections. Lastly we will use the site to undertake site-specific activities outside of what is happening at the galleries".

Sandy recognises that the website will create commercial dot com opportunities that couldn't be achieved through traditional media. As the site becomes more ubiquitous on a global scale he believes it may incorporate Web-based educational projects.

For the many not just the few

"We are currently planning two commissions for work that will be seen exclusively on the site. We hope to develop interactivity with some artists. One of our challenges is to show artists that the Web is not a threat but another valid avenue for the public to appreciate their work."

All the work to date on the re-launched site has been achieved on a very tight budget without an army of Web designers. "The whole first phase has been built on very small inputs of cash. I would advise others with great intellectual properties but little resource to firstly build a popular site, then the rest will follow by word of mouth."

Thanks to Sandy and the team, the Tate online project has proved a tremendous success in more ways than one. "While I don't think our website will change traditional forms of being creative, it will enhance the understanding and appreciation of works of art."

With visits from 143 countries and a reputation reaching further parts of the world, the site provides anyone who could never have the chance to visit one of the bricks and mortar Tate Galleries, with the opportunity to view some of the finest examples of art in the world. That's certainly a new twist on the term 'from canvas to screen-print'!

"While I don't think our website will change traditional forms of being creative, it will enhance the understanding and appreciation of works of art."

VP of New Media for EMI
Recorded Music, Jeremy
has travelled a long way
since 'The Raft' was the
first major music website,
and he has been
expanding the revolution
ever since, creating a
vibrant online music world

jeremy silver

eMusic maestro

emigroup.com

Jeremy Silver, VP of New Media, EMI Recorded Music, is a man of all seasons; past, present and future. It was back in 1993, an Internet lifetime ago, when he first linked himself with the Net. In his capacity as Virgin Records' Head of Press and Publicity, he came across a copy of *Wired* on a trip to the United States. On his return home, one of his first Internet adventures was to check out, from the comfort of his bedroom, university libraries in the States.

It was a revelation. Especially that the Internet contained 30 second music snippets. Fired with enthusiasm and demonstrating the prescience that would come to characterise his career, he made presentations to the Virgin board. By the end of 1994 he started to work on his first website named 'The Raft' from the book *Snowcrash*, a title well read in wired circles; it was to become Europe's first major music website.

Never mind surfing, try rafting

'The Raft' was a Heath Robinson affair – long before the Web ever existed. With the help of Paul Sanders of State 51, Jeremy cobbled it together. Accepting Jeremy's hint that the website was intended for research, the Imperial College allowed him access to the university network. Sun provided the hardware and Videotron laid the cable that connected it.

Narrow band transmission

'The Raft' went live in March 1995, immediately attracting a high traffic volume. At first, the website offered a limited selection of bands from Virgin's roster, most of them at the cutting edge of music technology, such as Future Sound of London and Massive Attack.

By the Autumn of 1995, Jeremy accepted the position of VP of New Media at EMI Recorded Music. After putting several CD-ROM projects 'to sleep', he concentrated on expanding the revolution he had started with 'The Raft'.

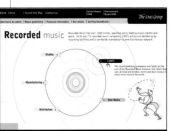

Power to the people!

Indeed it was a revolution. So much so, the establishment he master-minded in the music industry was closely followed – and often copied – by competitive corporates. Jeremy acknowledges the fascinating similarities between music and information. "Both are easily digitised. Both are simple to move around and built on hype. Young, white males heavily populate the music and information space." Jeremy points out that Internet engineers buy a lot of music. However, of particular interest, "Both groups create a sense of interaction, a feeling of community and a level of emotion belied by its manufactured format".

Jeremy is intrigued and in contrast appaled by the impact the Internet has had on the music industry. Those involved have virtually monopolised the way music is available directly online which in turn has transformed the way people engage in it. The playlist is the combination of musical consumption and management, which has produced a degree of personalisation many e-commerce magnates would die for.

"Luckily most bands consider the Web to be very cool, despite being on the road so much that they have no time to get their heads round it."

They're all a bunch of Net-heads...

In their own field, artists generally welcome new opportunities to pursue and practice their vocation. Jeremy maintains, "Luckily most bands consider the Web to be very cool, despite being on the road so much that they have no time to get their heads round it". In fact, keen to introduce his bands to new technology, Jeremy attempted to give them digital cameras to take 'candid' backstage snaps that could be posted onto the Web. Unfortunately, they proved too candid for Internet consumption! Another wheeze was to scan the contents of the bands' pockets when they arrived at the EMI office. Needless to say, that didn't last long either.

Despite these shortcomings and successes, Jeremy is in fear of some of the long-term implications. As he puts it: "It would be a tragedy if we have created a vibrant, exploded music world – while musicians are finding it more and more difficult to make a living. What future have musicians, now that music is available free on the Web?"

Jeremy has set his mind and attention to find the answer to that potentially suicidal question. Meanwhile he's letting the e-times roll.

As a musician, performer and songwriter, David Bowie continually reinvents himself and his art. After living each legendary character to the utmost, he deconstructed that which made him singular, then a new element would arise to confound and entice the masses who thought they had just figured out his latest incarnation.

david bowie

Musician and Web visionary

davidbowie.com

Recently Bowie, named as one of the top 20 visionaries of the 20th Century by Computer World, embarked on a revolutionary online journey which allows fans and Internet enthusiasts to enter his own private domain BowieNet, which was set up in 1998. Prior to this however, David had been experimenting with new technology, being the first rock artist to conduct all 'on tour' business communications by email on the Serious Moonlight Tour back in 1983. He was also one of the first name-brand artists to release a single online, with the 1997 track 'Telling Lies'. He commented, "I couldn't be more pleased to have the opportunity of moving the music industry closer to the process of making digital downloads available as the norm and not the exception." He has even experimented with CD-ROM versions of songs, which enable the user to create videos to accompany the music. As if this is not enough he has also pioneered the use of Web-casts and chats.

BowieNet offers so much more than an Internet connection, with rare audio tracks, video clips and backstage footage, live video feeds from the studio, live chat with David and his featured guests, an online journal and much more.

In addition to all of this David has also set up a website on which to display his own artwork and that by other contemporary artists. At bowieart.com you can purchase David's work online using your credit card or via an email. He has great plans to further develop the art website in the very near future, which will incorprorate an E-zine featuring interviews with artists and reviews of exhibitions.

David Bowie is also a Co-founder of UltraStar, a high-intensity affinity group Internet Company. As an online pioneer, UltraStar offers a subscription based revenue model for affinity group content, community and commerce. To date, the company specialises in bringing major entertainment, sports and fashion entities to the consumer Internet world in a community-based forum. By partnering project management with Internet technology, the company offers its clients full-service website development, including: Internet Service Provider launches, personalised email addresses, proprietary membership content, streaming video and audio, digital photography, discounted merchandise offerings and a host of additional online marketing and promotional services.

Ultrastar's corporate mission is to offer Internet users an up-close and personal look into specific interest niches by maximising the Web's interactive capabilities and community offerings. The company provides virtual gateways to the private and public lives of famous people, celebrated musicians, sports enterprises and headlining organisations. Leveraging the company's personal relationships with each of its client partners, UltraStar secures exclusive input, content and materials for its online properties and Web-based user groups.

Other proteges of UltraStar include The New York Yankees who after partnering with UltraStar were able to provide Yankee fans the most dynamic Internet-based community to interact, intertwine and even meet the all star team. In addition to the 1999 World Series ticket offers and play-by-play updates, YankeesXtreme.com provides Internet dial-up access. Based on the subscription to the Yankee network, the fans will have access which includes exclusive content, chats with players and coaches, digital photos and live cams, special merchandise, contests, 10MB of free web space, full access to the World Wide Web, bulletin boards and news groups and even customised Yankee email addresses.

"We feel we can add the same excitement and sense of community to Brownsonline which has brought so many music fans together at BowieNet. We couldn't be more pleased to be associated with this first class franchise."

Similarly in partnership with the Cleveland Browns, Ultrastar offers Browns fans full service nationwide Internet dial-up access, including email exclusive content including chats with players and coaches, digital photos and live cams, special merchandise and ticket offers, contests, 10MB of free Web space, full access to the World Wide Web, bulletin boards and news group.

Discussing the partnership David Bowie said, "We feel we can add the same excitement and sense of community to Brownsonline which has brought so many music fans together at BowieNet. We couldn't be more pleased to be associated with this first class franchise."

Other recent signings include the rock group Hanson and the world's leading Christian community leader Bill Gaither.

Further major new signings from the worlds of sport and entertainment are expected in the next three months.

Julie Howell, the name and face behind Jooly's Joint, is one of our greatest heroes. Her site is visited regularly by 10,000 members who are living and surfing with multiple sclerosis.

julie howell

Jooly's Joint: e-supporter extraordinaire

mswebpals.org

When did you first get involved in the Net?

In 1995. I love experimenting with new technology, finding out what it can do for me. The Web was just getting off the ground in the UK and I wanted to be a part of it. Not as a passive voyeur, but as an active contributor! I was keen to discover how this new medium could help people like me. At that point I had been living with MS for five years, but felt isolated and ill-informed. The Web struck me as a great way to put people in similar situations in touch. I found myself with half a megabyte of free Web space, Internet Magazines' HTML tutorial and a wild idea for an online community for people with MS. Five years on 'Jooly's Joint' has 10,000 members worldwide.

What is your greatest achievement?

I have managed to maintain the service for five years and amassed 10,000 members on extremely limited resources. Jooly's Joint survives on the kindness and generosity of people who lent me their expertise and resources when the service was in its infancy. The MS Society gave me a grant for a computer (I initially ran the service from a loaned one) and ISP Eurobell provide free Web hosting.

Key behind site?

I think it must be the personal touch and tender loving care that I have been able to give to Jooly's Joint. The site has my fingerprints all over it! People seem to feel a connection with me, and quickly give me their most precious gift – their trust. Through thoughtful use of colour, tone and graphics I have tried to create a positive environment that is full of hope and inspiration. The intention is not to trivialise MS, but to show that life can still be wonderful. Many newly diagnosed people come to the site, which is why it is so important to present the disease in a positive light.

How is it unique?

I think the site sets itself apart from other sites about MS because I do not publish information or advice - the service is simply a means for people with MS who are feeling isolated (and those who aren't) to meet others. At Jooly's Joint you will find no misinformation about MS, no cure-of-the-week fantasies, no false hope. The service is purely a platform from which people with MS can empower themselves and each other through the simple act of sharing.

What are your three top tips for building an Internet business?

1. Make sure everyone can use your site, including people with disabilities who might not be able to see the screen, because these are the people who stand to gain the most from access to your service.
2. Keep the navigation clear and consistent. This will build up user-confidence and keep them coming back (this is why Google is now my favourite search engine).
3. Resist the temptation to implement new technologies soon. Be sure to take your audience with you, don't leave them behind. People don't like change and become frustrated when they can't find what they need quickly.

How did you secure finances?

The MS Society have been hugely supportive and have helped me pay my phonebills and other Internet costs (which were hefty before the days of the free ISP). These days, the only running cost is my time, which I will always give freely. Some businesses have donated competition prizes in exchange for advertising. This helps everyone: it brings more people to my site, gives people with MS the opportunity to win something useful, and gives business access to a targeted market (on our terms!).

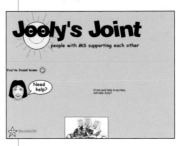

Any advice for other start-ups?

If you have a unique idea, don't waste any time, go for it! When I had the idea for Jooly's Joint back in 1995, there was very little on the Web for people with MS. Now all the good ideas seem to be in use!

Advice for traditional business?

The Web provides a fantastic opportunity for you to reach new customers. I know so many people with disabilities who are unable to get out to the shops, but who spend, spend, spend online. Don't under-estimate the value of the 'disabled pound' – exploit it!

Your vision for the Web's future

I dream of 'Internet everywhere'. Jooly's Joint attempts to be a cure for the isolation many people with MS feel. I've been in crowded places, and felt so alone with my problems. How wonderful to be able to take out my mobile phone and start chatting online to people with MS, friends or strangers.

Golden opportunities

The power of the Web to give a voice to the voiceless and community to the housebound.

How will you stay ahead?

By continuing to listen to the voices of the users of Jooly's Joint. New parts of the service are created all the time in response to requests from people with MS. I also hope to take the service to new platforms, to realise the vision of ubiquitos support. I would love for Jooly's Joint to be available via Interactive TV, public kiosks and mobile phones.

Any Net predictions?

I predict a more caring society. The notion that computers promote anti-social behaviour is false. Most people I speak to name communication as their number one reason for getting online. As services like Jooly's Joint are proving, increased communication can lead to better understanding and the discovery of common ground between people whose paths would otherwise never meet.

Personal hero

Tim Berners-Lee, inventor of the Web, for his vision and determination and his assertion that the Web is for everyone, regardless of ability or disability. Tim has put community before personal gain, and I respect that very much. I hope that what I am trying to achieve is in keeping with his vision.

Favourite sites

Because I'm so disorganised, lastminute.com is invaluable. Without it, I wouldn't have much of a social life! I'm very impressed by google.com, a fast and comprehensive search engine. icq.com is a fantastic communication tool.

Greatest thing about the Net

It is where personal homepages and corporate giants sit side-by-side. Ordinary people really can build new worlds through this medium, and we should all strive to keep the Net this way.

Worst thing

That spam and cyber-rage are rife. Email does not compare to face-to-face communication. Misunderstandings occur in cyberspace that wouldn't happen if tone and gesture could be conveyed.

"It is where personal homepages and corporate giants sit side-by-side. Ordinary people really can build new worlds through this medium, and we should all strive to keep the Net this way."

What inspires you?

The capacity of the human spirit to overcome adversity. I feel very blessed – each day I receive email from people who are dealing with the missiles life has launched at them. Some times people are down so low, but they endure.

I'm fiercely proud of the Jooly's Joint community, who rally round to set anyone who falls on their feet again. There is more laughter than tears, more pride than sadness and more peace than anguish here. How could anyone fail to be inspired?

What should inspire others?

That a modest idea can take flight. You don't need money or power to change people's lives. You simply need one good idea, a flexible approach, a love of change, empathy and lots of determination.

Soundbite

If I had to describe myself in three words, I would choose 'gregarious, infectious, unconscious'!

Any quirks or interesting facts?

At Jooly's Joint famous personalities mingle with the crowd. The common experience of MS – isolation, confusion, loneliness, self-doubt and fear as well as optimism and strength of spirit – unite an otherwise disparate group of people into a community.

Other interests

Life with MS isn't without its stresses, and I find music a great way to unwind. When your body is weak, you can live vicariously through the musical creations of your favourite artists. Just close your eyes and float away...

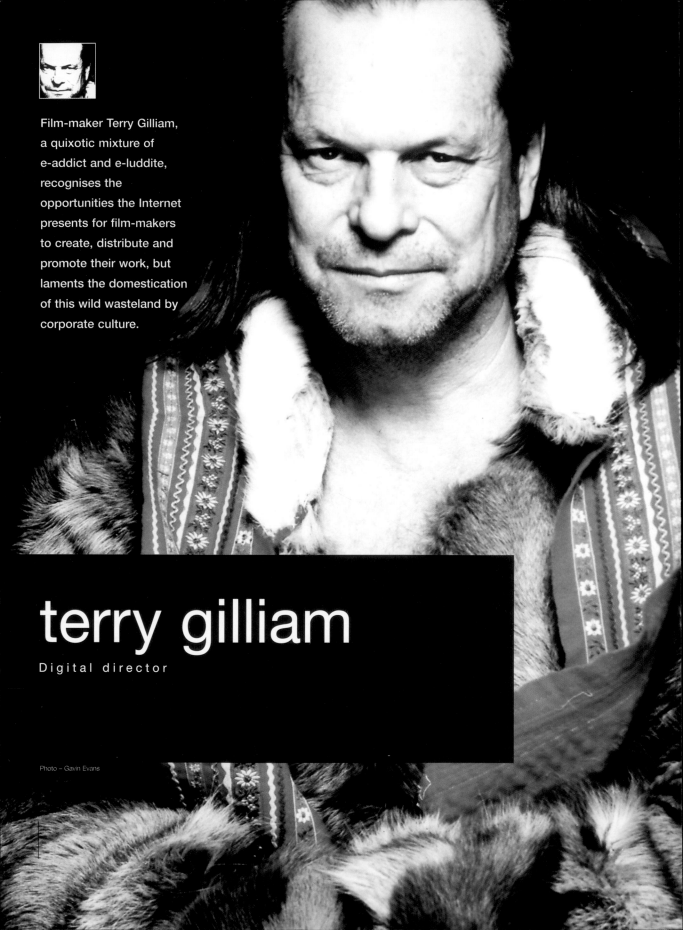

Film-maker Terry Gilliam, a quixotic mixture of e-addict and e-luddite, recognises the opportunities the Internet presents for film-makers to create, distribute and promote their work, but laments the domestication of this wild wasteland by corporate culture.

terry gilliam

Digital director

Photo – Gavin Evans

The meaning of life, the Internet and everything

Everyone familiar with the work of film-maker Terry Gilliam can testify to his distinctive perspective on the world. From Monty Python onwards, Terry's often surreal, consistently incisive vision, has given rise to fantasy as well as a fresh understanding of the meaning of life.

Terry has always done things on his own terms. He embraces the Internet enthusiastically but not unconditionally. He celebrates the Net's freedom, chaos, and humour, whilst respecting its darker side.

The propaganda network

Terry welcomes the Net's impact on the film industry – especially Hollywood. He cites the 'Blair Witch Project' as an example of bad pre-release hype emanating from the public, rather than Studio. Terry believes such lack of control worries Hollywood executives. "When Harry Knowles founded aintitcool.com, which published reviews from test screenings, Hollywood tried to co-opt him and suppress negative coverage," reveals Terry. "Hollywood wants mind control. The Internet offers an open mind."

Whilst the big film conglomerates stake their claim to the Internet, Terry foresees widespread clashes between corporate culture and opposing chaos. "As the Web becomes more consolidated, we'll receive an increasingly proscribed view of the world. The untameable will become domesticated and we will be the worse for it."

From imagination to digital image

On the other hand, Terry acknowledges that the Internet has had a beneficial effect on film-making. "New media technology is giving traditional and current film-makers alike the chance to create and publish work in ways that were simply inconceivable a few years ago," says Terry who has used digital technology since the movie 'The Fisher King'. Today he uses his digital camera, some editing software and an Apple computer to make complete (if, in his own words, 'rather crude') films.

Terry is so impressed by the opportunities which new media provides, that he encourages students to give up 35mm in preference for digital portfolios and calling cards. But, as he points out, "Technology can often do little more than enable a film-maker to discover his lack of talent faster".

Furthermore, as Terry explains, "The Internet (at least until the big corporates take over completely) offers an alternative outlet to budding film-makers whose work is rejected by, or unsuitable for, the big networks".

A cartoonist friend publishes Terry's work on one of the children's websites – and will continue to do so until parents complain about its patently adult, rather than childlike, content.

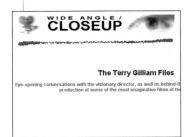

WIDE ANGLE / CLOSEUP

The Terry Gilliam Files

Eye-opening conversations with the visionary director, as well as behind-th production of some of the most imaginative films of th

WIDE ANGLE / CLOSEUP

The Saga of
BRAZIL

Terry Gilliam discusses the making and near-unmaking of his dystopian fantasy.

smart.co.uk/dreams

"Technology can often do little more than enable a film-maker to discover his lack of talent faster."

Furthermore, as Terry explains, "The Internet (at least until the big corporates take over completely) offers an alternative outlet to budding film-makers whose work is rejected by, or unsuitable for, the big networks."

Clearly Terry takes an ambiguous view of the Net. To his delight, it provides an environment in which mavericks thrive on originality and humour. "Where else but the Internet could pictures of 'women in casts' find a ready audience?"

Terry ruefully admits, "The Internet doesn't necessarily set us free". He spends more time sending and receiving jokes than getting on with his routine life. While 'nonsense and gossip' drag him away from work, his computer screen has a powerful hypnotic effect, which he counteracts by keeping his PC between two windows, so he can flick his eyes back and forth to the real world.

The wired and the wireless

Determined to resist the all-encompassing lure of what he describes as the 'e-ther', yet keen to harness its opportunities, Terry is a quixotic mixture of e-commerce addict and e-luddite. This man who became hooked by the dazzling bargains on the e-Bay auction site, yet often takes a month to reply to emails in deliberate defiance of today's instant-response culture. He loves books and the tactile experience of reading, yet buys them on amazon.com. And while he often retreats to his totally un-wired house in Italy to escape from the painful condition of 'information overload', the Internet can have a curative effect too. Whenever he suffers from an attack of self-doubt, Terry looks up his 'Ego Collection' of websites dedicated to him.

The Terry Gilliam Worship Page is particularly recommended for its restorative qualities.

Beenz, the Web's own currency, is such a good idea, you wonder why nobody thought of it before. Thanks to founder Phil Letts' methodology of 'business at the speed of light' and his uncanny ability to be in the right place at the right time, Beenz now has a global base of over half a million users.

phil letts

Web incentive impresario

beenz.com

In the closing months of the last century, just when everyone was getting comfortable with the concept of electronic commerce and the Web as a source for acquiring low cost CDs, books, air tickets, holidays – and little else – somebody came along and offered something, well, different. On the Net, different tends to enjoy a greater visibility profiled against a stark wallpapered Web canvas littered with a paucity of ideas and anonymous initiatives. The different idea was to give the globally Webbed-up community its own e-currency. The concept's prime mover was Phil Letts, CEO of beenz.com. Since its launch in March 1999, beenz.com has captured a global base exceeding half a million consumers.

A more rewarding Net experience

"Like Yahoo!, another prime mover, Beenz has held the imagination of both the business-to-consumer market as well as the all important consumer," enthuses Phil. "For the first time the Net has a dynamic marketing tool which is totally unmatched by any other Web reward scheme."

Beenz features flavours of supermarket loyalty cards and Air Miles, yet was borne out of the frustrations and inadequacies of online marketing. Especially Web banner ads that in many cases still command little respect and even less attention amongst consumers. Phil's alternative, the prospect of earning Beenz, alters the dynamic between Web merchant and consumer. Through the incentive scheme, Web-based corporations can influence the behaviour and purchasing habits of the consumer.

Great dreams grow from small Beenz

Phil's global dreams for a more rewarding Web started in 1998 when he met new media business consultant Charles Cohen. Charles suggested a Web-based reward scheme built around a Net-based currency that would attract people to sites. Not only that, but once there, the incentive would be strong enough to encourage surfers to click on banner ads, then reward them as both visitors to a participating site and as purchasers of goods on the self-same site. Best of all, being exclusive to the Net, the new currency would encourage Web commerce activity across a vast portfolio of accessible and available products and services.

From the start, Phil and Charles made it seductively easy for consumers to load their Beenz account with valuable credit. Customers simply register on beenz.com's website, create their own account, and then access Beenz-enabled sites across the Web. Phil's prospects for the company are exceptionally good. "When measured by the number of consumers setting up Beenz accounts on a daily level, we're one of the world's Top Ten sites," explains Phil. "Soon we will become an IPO."

Raising cash and eyebrows in the City

Says Phil, "To kickstart the whole Beenz idea, we looked for only half a million dollars. To help secure it, we pulled together a detailed 50-page business plan with the accent on investing in people. We also presented a very detailed company prospectus and development plan, a detailed exposition of the Net currency concept, an excellent summary – and a funky cover. The funky cover was important because we all knew that perception is reality in the world of incubation and VC funds. So it made sense for the plan to be drop dead gorgeous from the front cover onwards!"

People, timing – action

"Our business methodology is called, 'business at the speed of light'. It's all about people, key people, being in the right place at the right time, a flat management style and key managers empowered to take the right decisions quickly."

Seeds for heroic growth

"My tips for anyone launching on the Web today is to research big time and then write a brilliant plan matched by a core team of four or five people. Don't just put 'e' in front of your Web name – think long and hard about branding, otherwise you'll be stuck with a Net turkey. Next, get going on the Net as fast as you can. The whole Web e-commerce drama is being played out as a modern version of a land grab, so if you want to be on the Net do it today – not tomorrow!"

Phil's advice for future dot com heroes certainly worked for him. Beenz.com is one of the Net's textbook launch successes. That's given Phil the biggest incentive of all. "We won't continue to win or remain first in our chosen market, unless we continually innovate, change our offering as well as motivate customers along with the people who work for us."

A global democracy

As for Phil's predictions for beyond 2000, he sees traditional businesses eating up the Internet. "ISPs, telcos and PC manufacturers will become more aggressive. Beenz.com is very lucky in that we've secured insight into a lot of businesses. We've also witnessed a big dichotomy between well-engineered and managed dot com operations versus the large bureaucratic, and poorly managed firms. The depth of change needed in these businesses will take ten years to pull through."

"There's a golden opportunity for traditional businesses which understand that the Net empowers customers and that the digital economy is unlike anything that came before. For those businesses which recognise how the Web changes people's lifestyles, reinvents our world and triggers global democracy, the medium offers a completely new communications paradigm."

Phil also recognises some downsides, "Like the slow access speeds, the Net infrastructures and the clutter. However, that's what you get when you have 10m websites. Maybe it's an anathema to all those Web and e-commerce champions but I believe that it's too easy nowadays to set up business on the Web simply by hanging off a search engine!"

Three pillars of strength

So what inspires Phil? "Building a great business. People. Success and my family." Phil's wife, Kara, who runs a gym on New York's Upper West Side, recently gave birth to a son – Sebastian. Both look forward to spending more time back in the UK – post beenz.com flotation – at the couple's Chelsea Embankment apartment over looking the River Thames.

Now, is that a good idea or what?

> "My tips for anyone launching on the Web today is to research big time and then write a brilliant plan matched by a core team of four or five people. Don't just put 'e' in front of your Web name – think long and hard about branding..."

Wherever you are,
Peter Kenyon of
Manchester United will
keep you up-to-date on
the state of play, with the
site that attracts over
6 million hits a month.

When and how did you first get involved in the Net?
About two years ago.

What triggered that?
We wanted to communicate cost-effectively with a world wide audience. To do so we worked with organisations who really understood the Internet market. Working alongside partners like Sun we were able to create a communication tool that built traffic.

In what way has the Internet helped you as a football club?
It supports our beliefs that we have a broad geographical brand. In fact, it continues to demonstrate the ethos with 75% of the traffic coming inside the UK.

What about the future?
Our MTV and Vodafone deal prove that partnering is the way forward. In terms of off-field activities, we see the Internet and the e-commerce opportunities it offers, as probably the single biggest opportunity for the team.

Look at it like this: if you combine the power of our brand with the opportunities provided by mobile telephony, along with the expertise of our partners, you can begin to see how we can be of value to our supporters wherever they are located – at home, on the move, or on holiday.

How will this affect your product portfolio?
Providing we build trust with our supporter base, Man Utd is happy to be an agent for a whole range of other activities.

peter kenyon

Football online

manutd.com

We've started to use it as a real two-way communication piece. Which, again we see as being beneficial, as we we can get new products to market build our brand.

What's your advice to businesses considering going on the Web?
Don't just concentrate on putting up a homepage. Try to understand your customer base, and the way that the Web can support your business activity to reach that customer.

What are your favourite websites?

To answer that one, I need to go back to the first time I used the Web: I used to live in the States. Each night at ten, along with my mates, I would dial up the UK papers to find out the latest football results. So my first real experience was all about acquiring information.

It still is – but on a wider basis.
For example, If I want to know something about one of my friends who is ill, I can use the Web to look up symptoms. Whatever I need, the Web is a fantastic knowledge resource.

What drives you?

The thrust of any branded business is the ability to know your customer. Today's technology means I can talk to a customer in Singapore as easily as Stratford. I couldn't do that 10 years ago.

The Web is part of an all-encompassing communications tool. The more you use it the more you want to use it.

Is the whole team behind the Web?

Like anything else you've got to be able to demonstrate how the Web benefits a guy in the ticket office as well as members of the board.

The biggest stumbling block that we face today is accessibility and using a keyboard. The minute it all gets converged on a friendly format like TV or telephone the better for everyone.

"Today's technology means I can talk to a customer in Singapore as easily as Stratford. I couldn't do that 10 years ago."

heroic strategies for success

Shaping today's dynamic business environment

Heroic strategies for success

The heroes profiled in this book have brought to life how to play by the new business rules and be successful in the networked economy. They are shaping today's dynamic business environment and setting about it differently.

How do companies move forward, how can you propel your career forward, how do you turn that dot com idea into a reality? From traditional businesses to start-ups, from your initial business plan to IPO, how do you embrace the Internet economy and become a market leader? The answers are scattered throughout the interviews in this book like gold dust – and to make it easier for you, here are five top strategies for success gleaned from our heroes' experience and soundbites.

The big idea

Great dot com businesses are founded on big ideas. You don't always have to be the first to market. Ironically, when last to market with an idea you have the hidden advantage of being in a position to compare it against the competition and out-smart them. The big idea goes through all parts of the business, as illustrated in Figure 1.

Develop your ideas. That flash of inspiration will carve you a niche and could make you a paper millionaire. Whilst opportunities are plentiful, with all the known hype it is easy to think you have missed out on the Internet boom. However, heroes demonstrate everything is possible.

This is just the beginning of the Internet boom, the future points the way to more new opportunities. The emerging market for anytime, anyplace, anywhere Internet access, from mobile phones to handheld devices to Web TV provides hundreds of new content-driven business gaps. With personal devices, content providers can tightly tailor the service they deliver to the customer. Think of the ability to manage your finances, pay your bills, update your diary and shop, all from the palm of your hand. From banking to retailing to outsourcing your domestic chores, the market is wide open for new ideas, banks, companies, supermarkets and so on, to build killer Web services that we have not yet thought of but will be delivered by the heroes of tomorrow.

Look at the opportunities and go for it. That big idea can be triggered by changes at home, at work or changes in your own personal perspective. Richard Spinks had the idea for Vavo, a portal for the older generation, when his father-in-law became a widower. The idea behind Beenz started, like so many others, when two like-minded entrepreneurs got together – Phil Letts and Charles Cohen's early discussions led to the creation of the Web's first online currency.

The big idea

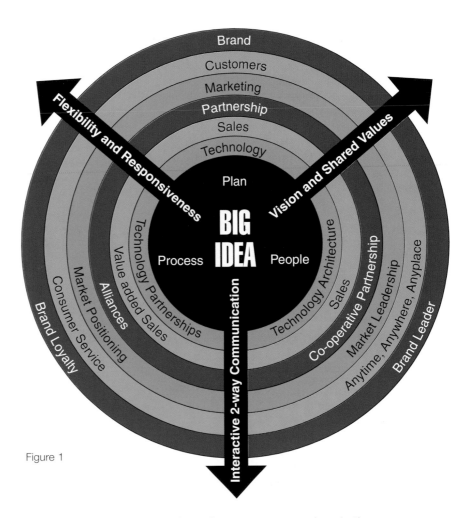

Figure 1

Get thinking – from market dynamics to your personal aspirations –
ideas can come from anywhere.

Think different, think beyond today, challenge existing thinking. The Internet is still evolving,
businesses could push change in a new direction, so your ideas can be wild and wacky.
Where will mobile computing take you and what will the impact of new technology be on
purchasing behaviour?

Simple ideas unite the founders, the employees and customers. From creating a
community for pet owners to selling books to uniting SME buyers and sellers, all the
founders behind leading sites have hit on the fundamental truth of successful business –
shared and connected values based on a big idea.

A shared vision and soul

One fundamental foundation to building a Web business is having a unified vision that underpins the whole company providing a set of shared values internally and externally.

In the new world, a business' 'shared vision and soul' is created by a strong and passionate set of values that everyone inside and outside the company can believe in. 'Soul' comes from company founders and the leaders who have a conviction in what they are doing. It's almost a religious vision that embraces everyone around the company and beyond, from employees, to suppliers, to customers. Having a 'soul' provides the finishing touch to the technology base upon which dot coms are built. Be wary: the pace of change, the power, the speed, the pressures of this technologically driven world reflect that the human side of life can be neglected.

Imagine working in a dot com and sitting behind a screen all day, all communications via email, mobile phones, pagers and digital television. By having passion and soul the founders of the successful dot coms provide personal fulfilment, team spirit, companionship and shared goals that balance the pressures of the Net Economy.

Companies have always had mission statements and strategic goals. However, the difference is the degree of energy and passion behind this new set of goals. Simulating a torpedo, every individual in this book from Brent Hoberman to Jeff Bezos, integrate the whole company behind a core set of values; Richard Branson's personal values are Virgin, the company is built around his character and persona. He has consistently performed differently, challenging the establishment when necessary. His online ventures like virginbiz.net reinforce this approach. Branson offers an alternative to small businesses in acquiring online service-orientated hosting at reasonable costs.

This vision clearly defines what the business is all about and where it is heading, rendering higher productivity and performance throughout the company. All are aware that their contributions can make a difference to the bigger picture. Thus, the combined dynamics of soul and vision justify the change in pace and how the phenomenon of Internet time is possible.

Be big! Be bold! Many of the new start-ups unashamedly aspire to worldwide brand domination, ownership of market segments. boo.com launched in a blaze of hype as the definitive worldwide online sportswear retailer. Sportal.com founded by Rob Hersov aspires to be the leading sports portal.

These challenging goals are not confined to the start-ups. Schwab.com had an explicit vision for the entire organisation to make dot com central with the bricks and mortar branches supporting online trading. Just as Hugo Drayton set up the Electronic Telegraph in 1997, he achieved his goal of establishing the UK's leading online newspaper.

These ambitious targets would not be achievable if not backed by a profound vision and shared values that transform the impossible into reality.

Building a dot com business

Despite the fact that dot com businesses are founded on technology, ironically getting your dot com idea online sometimes presents the biggest challenge. Technology can often be the stumbling block for many would-be dot com heroes. Terms like HTML, Web server, browsers, and networks can be intimidating. But don't worry. Your ability to set up dot com business reflects more on business skills than technical expertise. So long as you get the right partners behind you.

Drew Kaza – BBC

Today's new breed of business managers who drive the Net Economy are commercially acute, dynamic and visionary leaders; they are not computer nerds. You can find these new e-business managers setting up dot com start-ups and also in traditional businesses, re-launching existing business models – like Drew Kaza, the man behind BBC's highly successful beeb.com.

These Netrepreneurs are buzzing with new online business propositions. Even with recognised credentials, many entrepreneurs with exciting and strong business propositions fail to develop these initiatives because they do not know how to move forward from a technology perspective. The challenge is turning vision into a technical reality. New e-business visionaries have to bring their ideas to market faster than the competition. To deliver they have to build the IT infrastructure to support the business. Technology is the enabler.

Getting it wrong is not an option. In today's dot com world, the whole business model is built on technology. Slow download times, inadequate security and website downtime can destroy even the best business plan. Customers expect businesses to be online anytime, anyplace, anywhere. The minimum starting point is fast access to information, online support, easy processing of orders, responsive feedback and high security. To create genuine customer loyalty you have to go further with personalised content, offering order tracking, integrating online and off-line services.

Help is at hand for start-ups and business managers. With the world of technology ever changing, managers can no longer perform alone. Web-centric business requires the right partners to build the hardware, software and network infrastructure, which brings your idea to market.

Given the strategic importance of Web technology to every business, it is wise to have a basic understanding of how to build a successful dot com infrastructure. Figure 2 illustrates a framework to help you understand how to build a robust and scalable online business.

The dot com architecture

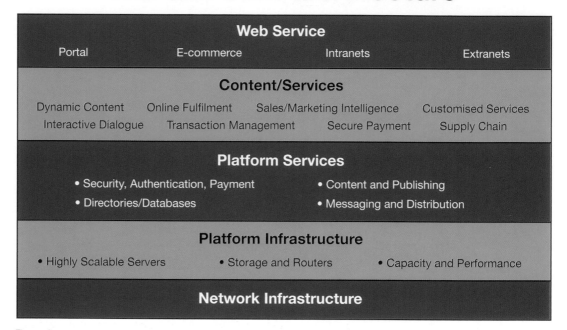

Figure 2

To build a solid dot com architecture, there are a number of simple design principles that you should follow. The heroes throughout the book demonstrate that by building your site based on a series of building blocks you will have a foundation for delivering high performance services that you can expand and evolve to match your needs.

The dot com building blocks are all based on well-defined public interfaces, easily controlled and manageable. From in-house developments to the increasing numbers of people who have outsourced their technology requirements to a service provider or those who have a strategy which combines both. But all of them share some common characteristics which provide scalability, uptime, security and performance.

Here are some points that you need to remember when building your dot com architecture.

– **Site design** Design a site which is customer focused, offering fast download speeds, simple navigation, secure, easy to use ordering, tracking and search facilities. They get the basics right.

– **Database services** To respond to customer needs you need to have a unified database strategy, where authorised users can all share data.

– **Public interfaces** All interfaces for each service should be formally specified and based on open industry standards, a consistent set of policies should be implemented to simplify management.

– **Security** The success and growth of e-commerce has increased customer confidence in the Internet. To build their trust you have to deliver a highly secure site with clear credit card, authentication and data protection policies.

– **Tiered architecture** For adaptability and growth implement a tiered and adaptable software and server architecture, implemented in layers. A high performance site will consist of a range of distributed servers, database servers, application servers and authentication servers.

– **Scalability** It is impossible to estimate how much traffic your site will generate. Many of our heroes totally underestimated the peaks in demand they would experience. From the start you need to build an open and scalable architecture and manage the server capacity so that you always offer high availability to your users.

– **Systems back-up** Ensure all data is backed up constantly on a remote site, a vital component of any disaster recovery plan.

– **Quality services** Manage and deploy quality network services that guarantee performance, availability and monitoring. A range of managed services are available to design, integrate and manage your dot com strategy and to deliver quality service.

John Beaumont – Planet. Online

There is a variety of affordable options. These are a range of Business Incubator programmes that give guidance, advice and access to a solid dot com infrastructure. Four companies that run one of these programmes are Cisco, Oracle, Sun and Exodus. Businesses can lease from them a range of hardware, software and network infrastructure at a fraction of the real cost all backed with expert consultancy and advice.

For a minimal investment you could also go to a service provider to set up and operate an interactive site. A new breed of service providers such as Planet Online and Exodus work with their partners, to offer a whole host of dot com schemes that provide the infrastructure to run an e-business, allowing you to focus on the core business.

Outsourcing your e-business hardware, software and network infrastructure needs is the way forward. Planet Online provides the technical support behind Freeserve, highlighting the fact that established businesses recognise that they offer better service, support, and time to market by outsourcing.

If you are behind one of the new hugely successful dot com start-ups, such as lastminute.com or qxl.com it is imperative that you have a reliable, scalable infrastructure that will let you grow with demand. By hosting with leading service providers the founders of both these market-leading sites know they can cope with surges in traffic and deliver the best performance to their customers.

The type of services being offered include ready built Web environments, Web design, transaction processing, security, site hosting and consultancy. By delivering a complete, cost-effective solution with secure, scalable and robust infrastructure dot com start-ups, including ready2shop.com have been bought to market in a matter of weeks. Or for even less cost you can set up as part of an established online shopping mall, where you can promote some products. Treat the project as a shop front, rather than building the whole outlet yourself.

There is a range of dot com consultancy services available, to help you define your dot com architecture, to reduce and even cure business headaches. It's a new type offering advice on planning, architecture and implementation expertise covering every area of the Internet from setting up a portal to e-commerce and service provision.

Provided by major system integrators, management consultancies and technology companies, these highly professional consultancies are widely available and in great demand. They help you build a complete service-driven site with many features such as auctioning, media rich content and personalised information, thereby ensuring you have the right infrastructure for elevated interaction.

Faster time to market, faster time to IPO and lower risks: sounds too good to be true. Yet the IT industry has woken up to the need to offer advice, planning and solutions to get your dot com idea online. Look for consortia of partners that can give you access to complementary services, experience and faster time to market. No one company can provide all the facilities, so look towards your service provider or chosen vendor partners to find your ideal solution.

Networked marketing

In the midst of all the dot com hype and media coverage, it is fundamental to develop a marketing strategy which takes your idea out to the market place and generates market share. From business-to-business to business-to-consumer, all the dot com heroes in this book have redefined marketing and created market share, creating customer focused brands.

Marketing is the key differentiator: a weapon that wins dividends, customer loyalty, and equally important, high stock market valuations. The explosive growth in dot com media spend highlights the 'market share' mentality. The goal is to win market share now and create a competitive block to new entrants. The aim is to create positive brand awareness and customer loyalty as fast as possible.

Historically, brands have been built and nurtured over generations, brands such as Coca-Cola, Levi, and Porsche. Today time is no longer a luxury we can afford. Marketing has to work its magic in a matter of months rather than years. So how do you market in the network age? Start by changing all your established marketing rules – dot com has to reflect the fundamental shift the Internet offers.

Ensure that all your communications have a clear and simple value proposition. State precisely what you are offering and what the benefits to the customer are. Many are still intimidated by the Web, while many others do not trust new names, so make it simple for customers to understand your value add.

Keep it simple, so avoid information overload, work overload and overexposed media hype. From every direction we are being hit by multi-messages so make sure you develop one that stands out from the crowd. Start with a cool, funky or descriptive Web address and follow this through all communication. Be personal and create a close relationship with customers. The days of mass marketing are dead. Today customers expect a high quality responsive service that makes them feel valued. Think personalisation.

Marketing has to be central to your business objectives. It provides a consistent and rewarding brand experience to your customers. From building awareness to handling customer enquiries, from delivering products and services to following up marketing, every one of these experiences has to convey the right messages.

Don't forget the basics – have a marketing plan, a clear target audience and well-defined processes, controls and budget management. Use the technology to collect information and build up a clear understanding and profile of your customers, based on profits. Then customise your communication so that your market messages tie into their needs.

Marketing strategies for a dot com era

Rethink how you deliver every part of your marketing. From events and fulfilment to press releases, everything can be dot com-med. Understand your target market and use the power of technologies to learn more about them. Be radical and reallocate your budgets to online initiatives: instead of a new brochure set up an online fulfilment section, host webchats, and webcasts, create online communities and email databases.

Mylene Curtis – virginbiz.net

Dot com marketing is about delivering a multi-dimensional campaign that gives customers a deeper understanding of what you do. Figure 3 (overleaf) illustrates that advertising is just one dimension of the mix and should be used to convey a clear proposition, not hype. Too many dot com marketing strategies are about creating short term pre-IPO brand hype without reinforcing this with strong content and a positive online experience. Integrate relationships, building techniques into your marketing; focus on customer service, building a community; encourage users to share views (the Tate Gallery has done this well), refer a friend campaigns, special promos, feedback loops, invest in marketing that gives rewards and a positive experience – these should be the basis of your marketing campaign and from here, build up clear values and propositions. Expand this philosophy through joint endorsements with partners via affiliation marketing, which is great for reinforcing the brand.

Dot com marketing is about more than just big budgets and cash, you need to go back to basics and a customer focused strategy that delivers content and creates a community to ensure brand loyalty.

Multi-dimensional marketing

Figure 3

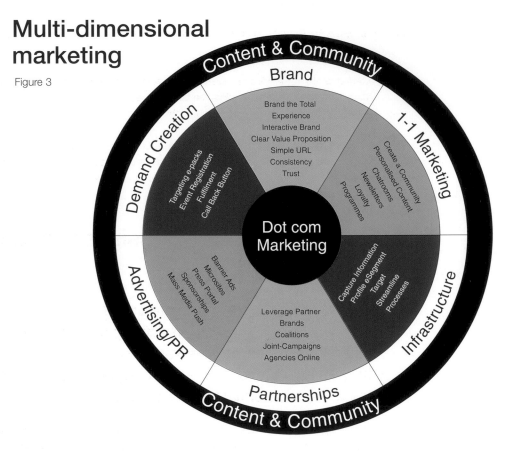

It is not a question of if you dot com but when. ACT NOW.

Points to remember when creating your dot com strategy.

Be Personal Keep close to your customers, give them personalised information and feedback. This is the best way to win brand loyalty.

Pick and Mix Ensure your marketing strategies are not one-dimensional. Combine the value of advertising with the power of PR and online and offline demand creation.

Power of PR The media is obsessed with dot com! Make sure you have a unique spin to give you coverage. Classic PR strategies work: photo stunts, glamorous, young, unusual, celebrity founders, niche ideas, new twists on old ways of doing things.

Collaborate marketing Leverage partner brands, from your technology partners to suppliers. Not only does this speed up the process of marketing but it helps you add a new dimension to your message.

Simple URL Get over the overload. Make it simple for everyone to understand what you are about.

Market share comes first Evaluate all the strategies to enable you to gain market share faster. This may mean 'influencing' the brand values, sometimes it's easier to gain market share with the masses and then push up the value chain.

The heroes profiled recognise that marketing is critical to success, they invest in the brand and ensure the marketing strategy has board level commitment. Just like the technology infrastructure, having a solid high impact marketing strategy will propel you forward.

The new dot com business models

The dot com age is about more than Web pages and employee email. It is about redefining every business function and changing the way you run the company from how to liaise with customers, employees and suppliers, to the design of products and IT strategies.

Today every business is part of the dot com era and has to evolve accordingly so that strategies integrate the Internet. Commitment has to come from the top, from founders of new companies to CEOs of existing traditional business. For example the *Financial Times* has transformed itself with FT.com, making use of core content but adding new values, delivering new services to customers. The network has to be at the core of every strategy. It's time to re-evaluate traditional business models, just as our dot com heroes have done, from setting up satellite dot com businesses, to re-defining how to use your core assets. Get your dot com strategy right and your balance sheet will benefit.

Transform your business by re-assessing the way you do business. Even if this means changing the very core of your success. Find new ways to add value to products and services. Add new online processes and controls to reduce costs and increase time to market. Re-think how you do business. The financial services sector has changed forever; moving from one-to-one selling to online sales as demonstrated by the success of Egg. If you are creating a dot com start-up, then from the outset ensure every function is online. From the start use technology as a competitive weapon with suppliers, customers and employees.

It's not a side show

Dot com is not a joke. It re-defines every aspect of business, from how you cope with suppliers to how you interact with customers. (this is illustrated in Figure 4 below) Traditional business functions have conspicuously changed. There is greater interaction across business both internally and externally. Firstly, recalculate your core strategy and goals, how dot com can help you perform differently. Secondly, re-examine how each department operates and delivers. This is the time to reallocate resources and realign assets behind new strategies.

Move your business online

Figure 4

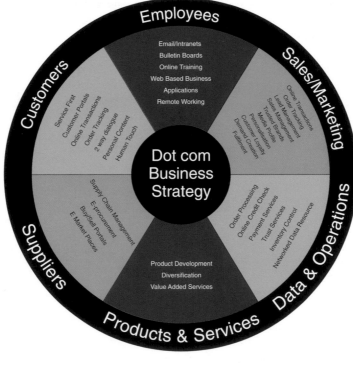

At the simplest level dot com-ming means moving business functions online. Automating bill payment and presentation, integrating suppliers and customers. All our heroes go beyond this. They recognise that the Internet can increase efficiency across businesses, providing the ability to buy at lower prices, reduce overheads and operating costs, generate the benefits of outsourcing. They integrate the Internet at the heart of their business strategy to increase efficiencies and generate a competitive edge.

Customers first

Competitive pressures are getting greater, global competition, the advertising brand wars, hundreds of new dot coms fighting for market share. It is getting harder and harder to attract customers, it is getting harder to be heard with all the advertising noise. This gives rise to two challenges, the first is to acquire the customer and the second is to maximise the revenue you generate from that customer.

Firstly you should dot com virtually all aspects of your interactions with customers, so that once you capture their attention you keep it. Create awareness on and offline and build loyalty by delivering a rewarding online experience, make it easy to conduct online transactions that offer supplementary services, deliver strong after sales services and loyalty programmes.

Whether you create a new Web team or extend the role of marketing it is strategically important to develop online content, manage the customer experience, user interfaces and retain a strong look and feel.

Customers should have direct access to your products, services and personalised information, whenever they want it, from any device they happen to be using. Ensure that every time a customer interacts with you online it is a positive experience. The site must always be available, secure, fast, easy and interactive.

Consumer dynamics have changed, time is of a premium, customers want to buy a range of goods from companies that they trust. Customers have become more demanding and the companies that are responding to this are winning. So once you have established a brand the future is to offer more to these customers, or create alliances that allow you to maximise the opportunities. Amazon's business has evolved from selling books to offering multiple services including CDs, electrical goods, videos and DVDs. In the world of publishing the Internet has delivered profound changes in terms of products and services companies such as Pearson, who deliver through FT.com adding value to the core news content.

Extended products and services

Another trend of the new economy is to extend the services that you offer customers. Given that it is so difficult to gain market share and customer attention, once you have attained this the key is to use it to your advantage

Chris Dedicoat – Cisco

The rise of the Internet has given rise to whole new range of products and services being offered. Companies that once had simple value propositions are now delivering more and more services. Many of those featured in the book are continually adding new services, from Excite to Lastminute to Amazon they all offer a greater spread of services now than they did six months ago and this is constantly evolving.

Providing a physical product or a single service is just the starting point, the opportunity that the leaders exploit is the follow-on sales, value-added services, creative partnerships and marketing that offer more.

The Internet gives you a chance to provide more personalised and customisable products, just as silicon.com's news does in the delivery of personalised content to IT professionals. By extending your offering you can generate incremental revenues, not just from direct sales, but from services and as the traffic increases so do your opportunities to generate revenues from other sources such as advertising or partnership deals.

Operational savings

The effective use of Web technology throughout the company can cut costs and result in operational savings. Cisco, Sun, Dell, Amazon are all global businesses that own their sector and they all have a Web centric business strategy which gives them a competitive edge. They use network computing to improve business processes, sharing information across the organisation.

By having networked systems where everyone can share information, it means everyone can be customer focused. Management reporting can be dramatically improved by providing instant access to sales data, customer satisfaction indexes, inventory levels. The key is to ensure the right information is accessible to everyone that needs it, when they need it – this means building a distributed computing architecture.

Unlimited information

Isolated islands of information which belong to specific departments, or individuals, as is often the case in a PC-centric business, make it impossible to share information. Scalability and responsiveness are hindered. By integrating discrete information resources together into a unified management system you create a valuable resource. It allows all parts of the company to work together, a system that gives a unified view of the customer, an approach that leads to design wins. By managing information via the network you create an intelligent infrastructure that provides the basis for delivering value added services. You create information resources that you can access from anywhere, quickly, so you can meet the demands of this fast changing economy.

Business portals

Just as we have seen the rise of consumer portals such as Excite and Lycos, there is now a rapid rise in business portals that provide personalised and niche content that generates benefits for even the most traditional business. Build Online, provides all the benefits of good project management online to the construction industry, creating relationships between suppliers, architects and builders. This is just one of a whole range of online services that can help drive down costs by matching buyers and sellers, or by delivering value added services.

This new type of portal, the business intermediary, like mondus, who assist in the search, evaluation and purchase of products and services for the small and medium sized business, make doing business easier. Improving the dissemination of information they are reducing costs and improving time to market for all their customers.

New world employees

In such a fast moving world you need fast moving innovative employees – attracting and retaining the best is mission critical. Success is about people, as demonstrated by everyone in this book. So what is so different about our heroes personnel strategies?

The dot com leaders attract the best because they offer the best – they strive to create a dynamic workplace. A place where everyone is united behind a set of shared values; hard work and dedication come from within not bureaucratic rules. Flexibility is the key, right down to new remuneration packages, share options, profit participation, competitive salaries and alternative work practices.

Remote working, giving employees access to all the information they need from home or a satellite workplace ensure companies are not restricted by geography on who they can recruit. Given the growing difficulty of recruiting high calibre staff, the value of contractors, portfolio workers who work for you part time and remotely offer huge benefits in terms of giving access to highest calibre skills.

Making resources and the right tools more accessible to every employee enhances productivity and job satisfaction. From the newest start-up to leading brand names they provide high performance access to Web technology from every desktop. By offering high-speed access to shared information, often housed in an open team-orientated environment employees can maximise their personal productivity.

And in a world that never sleeps the successful companies ensure that authorised users can access personalised information anytime. From emails to customer presentations, customer account details to sales data, car fleet or pension details, having access to all this material online is more efficient. Users access information when they need it, work when they want to.

Mark Suster– Build Online

Transforming supply chains

The way forward is for businesses to use the power of the network to transform supplier interactions. Several years ago we witnessed the advent of the supply chain, in which companies began sharing their product development plans with suppliers, channel partners, and manufacturers to ensure more timely delivery of new products. Today businesses of every size are using the Internet to take the concept of the supply chain a step further. For all businesses the Web gives critical information involved in developing, manufacturing, distributing and inventory management of products. Forward-looking companies are using the Internet/extranets to improve their interaction with suppliers.

Rouzbeh Pirouz– mondus

Business the next phase

As the Internet evolves it is adding efficiency to business at every level. New Web-centric businesses have reduced their cost structures and now traditional bricks and mortar companies are playing catch up by integrating the Internet and reducing overheads.

The dynamics of the Net economy means that business has to change. The growth, the low inflation, low unemployment, increasing demand for Internet savvy employees, the speed of change, advertising mania. In the first phase the Internet was customer facing; in the next phase it is having a dramatic effect on cost structures, product portfolios. With the rise of business portals and outsourcing we are seeing business strategies changing and the introduction of new business models.

Every industry, every manager has to move forward and play by the new rules. Companies have to understand that the future of the Internet is pervasive – this is just the beginning. The Internet affects every aspect of business. Those that shape the rules and use the Internet to evolve become more competitive and will be the heroes of tomorrow.

dot com strategy mapping

Dot com strategy mapping

All these featured in the book have a dot com strategy that is central to their business and clearly leveraged to give them competitive advantage which in turn increases their market dominance.

As a guide to helping you strengthen your dot com positioning, this dot com strategy mapping model helps you plot where you are now, how to move forward and how to make yourself more competitive. Dot com strategy mapping allows you to build a dot com plan of attack.

How can dot com strategy mapping help you?
– A tool to help you design and evolve your dot com strategy
– Simplifies dot com, giving you a clear picture of the dot com landscape
– Demonstrates clear opportunities and threats in the market
– Provides a framework to refine your business goals
– Highlights the dot com possibilities open to you
– Allows you to visualise the degree and extent of your dot com-med business
– Presents you with a range of new business models
– Highlights how well you have built a dot com infrastructure
– Gives you a framework to understand the competitive landscape
– Provides help in communicating your business goals

Whether you want to start up a new business or transform an existing one, dot com strategy mapping (as shown in figure 5) allows you to plot the different opportunities you have available to you. Through a clear understanding of your business you can arrive at a clear set of goals which highlight the power and potential open to you.

Figure 5

Dot com strategy mapping

Market position – this axis plots the relative market position of a company in terms of its market share, moving from small and medium companies operating in local markets to global multinationals. A low positioning, in the lower axis indicates lower market share. The mid-point indicates a stronger market position. Market coverage and share increase until the highest point on the axis, which represents market dominance.

Dot com architecture and strategy – this axis plots how central dot com is in the overall business strategy, it plots how well Internet technologies are being used to gain competitive advantage. An extreme position in the left-hand corner represents a company operating on traditional structures with legacy systems, limited integration and lack of networking capabilities.

A move along the axis represents greater integration of networked computing and open communications within the business strategy. At the mid-point dot com is delivering a core competitive advantage; this can be either in the front end in the form of a website and customer management systems or in more B2B area implementations such as supply chain management. On the far right-hand side are pure Internet-based businesses, whose core competency and business proposition revolves solely around the Internet.

Voyagers, Warriors, Explorers and Pioneers

Dot com Voyager
Voyagers are generally larger companies moving from the old economy to the new economy, they have to learn to compete in the vast new world of dot com facing the new challenges, cultures and new business models needed in order to remain competitive. The characteristics of a Voyager usually include:

- Well-established brand, with strong asset and resource base
- Clear value propositions and product/service offering based on old economy
- Often need to re-align culture behind the new dot com business rules
- Need to empower staff, speed up decision making and free up resources
- Need to integrate dot com into business strategy across key business functions
- Employees' communication, operations, manufacturing, supply chain management, customer management, marketing, sales can all benefit from the networked age
- Need to integrate legacy systems, recognise the value of outsourcing and focusing on core competencies

Dot com Warrior
Warriors are those companies whose vision and strategy is founded on dot com and their established market leadership is maintained through brand wars and positive associations. The characteristics of a Warrior usually include:

- High brand values which are highly associated with the dot com age
- Board level commitment to the Internet, a set of values which prevails across the company
- Internet technologies and the power of the Internet recognised in the core business strategy
- Global or multi-market coverage
- Recognise the need to maintain continuous innovation and maintain momentum
- Integration of on- and off-line business strategies is critical to success
- Recognise the power of partnerships and alliances to maintain market strength.

Dot com Pioneer

Pioneers are the developers who are creating the new dot com landscape, always innovating and introducing new ideas, new models and new ways to compete – all based on a dot com strategy. The characteristics of a Pioneer usually include:

– Highly innovative dot com focused business with growing market domination
– Dot com is at the very core of the business strategy
– Vulnerable to investor predictions and moods and new competitive attacks
– Establishing market share is critical in order to create barriers to entry
– Recognise the importance of establishing customer loyalty
– Creating strong alliances and partnerships is key to success
– Grab market share and make huge investments in brand and market positioning
– Outsource technology infrastructure and focus on core competencies
– Focus on content and ability to deliver service

Dot com Explorer

These are companies that are founded on traditional business models and who are now experimenting in the unfamiliar dot com world. The characteristics of Explorers usually include:

– Under increasing competitive pressure and can gain huge benefits from integrating dot com
– Create a Web presence via a service provider so can focus on core business
– May have limited inhouse technological expertise and dot com knowledge
– Strengths based on a core product/service rather than dot com
– May have limited resources, in terms of cash and skills organisation
– Vulnerable to growing competitive pressures

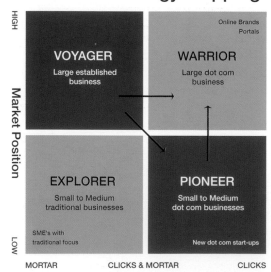

Figure 6

Voyager to Warrior (Figure 6)

There are a number of simple steps that can be taken to ensure dot com is central to the strategic direction of even the most traditional business. Someof the strategies adopted by the heroes include:

– Set up an online version of your core business
– Start re-inventing your core business functions and dot com everything
– Create a new dot com division with autonomy and flexibility
– Acquire a dot com business
– Partner with a dot com business

Dot com strategy mapping

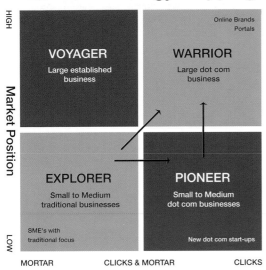

Figure 7

Explorer to Pioneer or Warrior (Figure 7)

Moving from start-up mode to market dominance would have been viewed as unthinkable ten years ago. But today putting the right dot com spin on even the simplest idea can transform you into a global player. Some of the strategies adopted by the heroes include:

– Start by dot com-ming your customer relationships, offering online access to your existing products and services
– Create a positive Web experience that improves customer loyalty
– Choose the right service provider to help get online easily, delivering quality services cost effectively
– Create alliances and partnerships to move into dot com space
– Become part of the value chain to a strong dot com business by providing the back end products or services need
– Start to dot com parts of your business to improve communication, reduce costs and enhance communications

Dot com strategy mapping

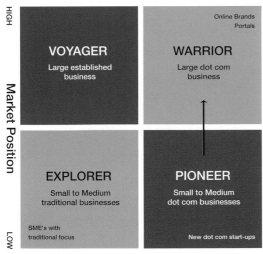

Figure 8

Pioneer to Warrior (Figure 8)

A dot com strategy is not limited by borders to regions, only your ability to deliver. Moving a clicks-only company to compete on the international stage can deliver huge rewards. Some strategies adopted by the heroes include:

– Bring the clicks to the bricks, by establishing a complementary partnership with an established business to leverage brand associations and sales channels
– Clicks to clicks, form partnerships with other dot coms to strengthen strategy
– Create dot com alliances and partnerships to move you into new markets
– The dot com world demands market dominance so invest in market growth
– Build the brand and evoke a clear value proposition with customers
– Secure resources and go for aggressive marketing campaign
– Be acquired or have an acquisition strategy to accelerate growth in the dot com space
– Leverage your partners brands and marketing to push you forward.

Warrior remaining as Warrior (Figure 9)

Staying at the top is the most difficult of all business challenges. To stay ahead you must be one step ahead of the game. Some of the strategies adopted by the heroes include:

- Always put the customer first
- Continue to innovate and offer new services
- Maintain and champion a dot com culture
- Acquire innovative start-ups
- Diversify into complementary clicks & mortar companies
- Honour and protect the brand
- Use size to create barriers to entry
- Maximise the opportunities of everyone wanting to share in your leadership success
- Hold onto your best people
- Continue to forge partnerships and alliances and build on existing ones
- Integrate backwards into Bricks and Mortar to strengthen your online offering.

Watch your back!

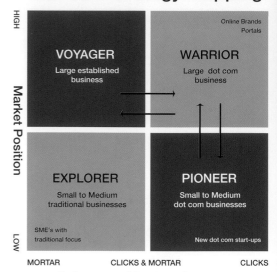

Figure 9

Dot com strategies that deliver results

Whatever your position on the dot com strategy map, its important to recognise this is just the beginning and that every company has to continually evolve, dot com is the future and everyone can learn from our heroes who set out some simple strategies for success.

- Dot com and win, embrace the Internet, this is the future
- The board should have a dot com strategy to stay in business
- Get started now, whether big or small the key is to start evolving
- Build a trusted brand and reinforce these values online
- Empower your best people to dot com your business
- Put customers first and exceed their expectations
- Use the Internet to re-define how you do business
- Develop strong partnerships and alliances
- Build a scalable, reliable dot com architecture that will grow with you

101 ways to be a hero

101 Ways to be a dot com Hero

You've learnt the big steps to get you on the way, now here's 101 practical hints and tips that have contributed to the success of our profiled heroes.

ACT IN INTERNET TIME

"Do not neglect the Internet – it is not a leap of faith, but a vital business consideration."

Ron Dennis, West McLaren Mercedes

1   **Dot com now**
The world has changed, embrace the Internet now with an open mind and passion, like all the heroes.

2   **Internet time rules**
Remember, in Internet terms, a three-month period is equivalent to a year in traditional business. From vision to reality, prevailing ideas go from inception to implementation in a matter weeks not months – an issue big business has to address. ThinkNatural.com launched in four months which is now the average time from idea to launch – so get moving fast!

3   **Every second counts**
In the Internet age the world never stops. It is a global market and someone somewhere will always be awake and ready to surf. Your business has to put the customer first every second of the day.

4   **No red tape needed**
Big business often holds back personnel by red tape and bureaucracy. Dot com companies have dynamic 'go-for-it' management that achieve results.

5   **No comfort zones**
Many employees have lost a sense of purpose and career direction. They have been caught up in administration. They are left stranded, unmotivated, just getting by in a comfort zone. Give them a vision, a clear set of aims and goals to induce their hidden talent and 'hey presto' they will deliver results.

6   **First mover advantage**
Acceleration to market and winning the race are essential to success. Common trends include faster time to market than competitors, such as transferring an idea from one continent to another, often at the expense of the original founder.

7 Last mover advantage

With the benefit of hindsight, watching and learning from the competition provides added value beyond what is currently available, leading to numerous new marketing opportunities.

GET STUCK IN

"It's all to do with pace, innovation and creativity."

Brent Hoberman, Lastminute

8 Attitude counts

Adopt a predatory attitude, attack the market and grow. You can take on the big guys and win. The starting point is self-confidence to attain market reach. With 10,000 new website names being created daily, it becomes virtually a prerequisite that you acquire a permanent hold before someone else brings in their marketing muscle and dominates you.

9 Innovate continually

In aiming for success, you need to innovate continuously. Supplement your offering, motivate staff with improvements, and last but not least aim to exceed customers' expectations.

Do not wait for permission and concensus, but embrace change, just as Excite do with their "leap before you look" philosophy.

10 Use what you know

Exploit fully your existing knowledge to achieve success rather than enter an unknown new field. Add a new spin to your core skills through adding the dot com advantage, which the Tate Gallery demonstrates, depends on content and passion more than cash.

11 Build strong alliances

Work with partners sharing your vision, ethics, and values, collectively propelling you into the limelight faster. The right partners lead to mutual benefit, especially in areas where your own knowledge is weak. Even short-term results are achieved faster with the co-operation of fellow partners.

12 Serial entrepreneurs

It is fallacious to assume you can only have one great idea. With support, you can make many dreams come true.

CUSTOMERS COME FIRST

"Our vision is very clear. We are on the customer's side."

Mike Harris, Egg

13 Customer focused

Don't just listen to customers, put them first. Consider the use of available new technology. How does it all enhance your vision? Can you provide services that customers didn't even think possible?

14 Open conversations

Technology encourages two-way conversations between employees and customers. Web-based communication is faster – more informal – giving rise to greater honesty. Companies cannot cower behind bureaucracy. Today's customers seek a dialogue with your organisation.

15 Brave words

Customers' fingers get brave when they hit the keyboard, often making demands they would never suggest on the phone. Be ready with a rapid response. Moreover when backed with email or a phone call, this can work wonders for customer satisfaction.

16 Instant satisfaction

Customers want instant response and delivery of services 24/7. Personnel have to recognise this, placing the customers first, backed by systems that ease pressure and increase response.

17 Corporate firewalls

Companies cannot hide behind corporate firewalls. Customers expect immediate interaction so provide real knowledge exchange and customised responses.

18 Networked customers

Customers in networked markets are better informed and share company product and service information with other customers. One mistake could be shared across a global market so get it right first time.

19 Consumer touchpoints

Customers have many means to keep in close contact with your company: from the Web experience, to the telephone to physical shops. The key to customers' loyalty is by harmonising all these points of contact, making it enjoyable for the customer to do business with you.

20 Consumer technology

Customers have access to an ever increasing range of technology, from labour saving devices to new communication tools. By means of mobile phones, email, palm pilots, Web TV, your site increasingly has to be accessible from anywhere. Build them into your strategy.

21   Get the content right

Richard Spinks of vavo.com advises, "Hand over the decision of site content to the people who are going to use it". Vavo has excelled in satisfying loyalty, reflecting the wishes of customers. So focus on delivering value added content.

22   Personalisation

Utilise the Web to the utmost by delivering richly personalised products and services to businesses and consumers. All businesses, both large and small, now can talk to their customers as if in a one-to-one conversation. Customers want to feel you are talking to them individually – not on mass.

23   Customer understanding

Get to understand your customers through conducting online surveys, or online focus groups and speaking to them in chat rooms. The Internet is perfect for gathering qualitative and quantitative data. Use that benefit to your advantage.

24   Branded experience

Your customers' experience on your site should reinforce your core values. Every department and partner inside and outside your organisations needs to understand this.

HEROIC PERSONALITY TRAITS

"Commitment is one of the keys to a successful Internet business."

Bob Davis, Lycos

25   Obsessive natures

Call it perfectionism or obsession, but all the personalities behind the Net are totally committed to their chosen mission. They crave challenges and have boundless energy. If this sounds like you, maybe we should have your name for the next edition of this book!

26   Be passionate and let everyone know it

Natural enthusiasm and passion unites everyone in this book. Passion assumes many guises, leaping out instantly as experienced with Brent Hoberman from lastminute.com. For others it seeps through, gradually revealing itself as with Mike Harris at Egg.

27   No boundaries

Operating day and night at Web speed, the boundaries dividing work and play cease to exist. It is a world where work is play and play is work. The old-fashioned practice of putting life into neat little compartments is well and truly over.

28   Accept knockbacks

You're living in a world where consensus management for funding and endorsing an idea is no longer practised. What counts is a self-belief to forge ahead, even when others can't fully grasp your vision. Don't expect total support. Take calculated risks, even when others are trying to hold you back.

29 True to yourself

Pete Goss declared, "People need a true to themselves attitude. It doesn't just have to be about climbing Mount Everest. It's often the small things that release the hero inside us." Go climb – get out there!

30 Play by new rules

True to themselves, dot com heroes break away from the traditional management mould. As individuals they operate on their own terms. Netrepreneurs dress with personality rather than wear corporate uniforms, their words are not rehearsed but a natural stream of consciousness. It's time to throw away the old rule book.

31 Soul mates unite

The making of outstanding management teams derives from the strength of the individual heroes and how they surround themselves with other likeminded individuals. The underlying truth is that the majority of dot coms are built by a group of founders and teams that truly respect each other and have complementary talents.

32 Be a media luvvie

The Internet brands of today, such as Amazon, Egg, eToys, Yahoo! and Excite have dramatically changed the profile of business-people in the media. Kajsa Leander at boo.com and Jeff Bezos at Amazon typify them and the media is hungry for their story.

33 Get ready for the burn out

Live for today; enjoy the buzz, it's a hyperactive gold rush; a 24-hour party. But the wise are shrewd enough to realise that the spotlight will eventually fade. So make time for the softer side of life.

HEROIC BUSINESS – THE NEW RULES

"Think radically about new business models."
John Beaumont, Planet Online

34 Anytime, anyplace, anywhere

If you've got it, the Web has the technology to deliver it, anywhere via a growing range of media devices. Use that technology and think anytime, anyplace, anywhere on anything.

35 Think multiple channels

Today, channels to market can mean paper-based catalogues, direct selling, telesales, digital TV, mobile phone, Internet. The key is to integrate the right components into your strategy.

36 Open and honest

Foster an air of openness, thereby encouraging people to share ideas to become innovative. Try out new techniques that make employees use their own initiative.

37 Multiple Revenue Streams

Be innovative in how you generate revenue, introduce new revenue streams, charge for online services, offer pay-to-view options, introduce subscriptions, offer microsite sponsorships and increase advertising revenue.

38 Deliver new services

The Web provides new opportunities for businesses to deliver radical new services. For example, in business-to-business computing, companies are increasingly outsourcing their buying requirements to online organisations. Even software is available on tap. Consider offering a buying service to consumers, pin-pointing the best products at the best price. Infomediary portal sites demonstrate that the Internet is a catalyst of business change.

39 Management diversity

Strong diverse management teams with skills embracing finance, marketing, sales and technology. One-dimensional teams with tunnel vision cannot create breakthrough strategies. Boardrooms should be full of lively discussion, not sleeping executives.

40 Dot com your established business

The Web changes the ways customers, employees and suppliers engage with each other. Companies have to change everything from the way they network to their goals for expansion.

41 Re-define products and services

The dot com age facilitates quick and effective delivery of products and services. For example, the Hilton Hotel Group costs for online reservations are just pence compared to pounds through more traditional channels such as agents.

42 Dot com executives

Raise your conservative corporate executive to the dot com world. In doing so they will revitalise their world and your business.

43 Get started

Dot com is evolving and will constantly change business patterns. Even in the absence of a complete strategy, get yourself started with dot com-ming parts of your business from salespeople on the road to developing new business models.

44 Blurred boundaries

Accept that the boundaries between, inside and outside businesses are blurred; get set to develop fresh opportunities, which benefit suppliers, employees and customers.

45 Breakout

Be a rebel, traditional or untraditional. Ahead of you are opportunities aplenty. Vitalise your career with creativity. Give yourself a fresh type of individuality.

46 Old world new world

Not uncommonly, many CEOs and executives have to manage old and new businesses simultaneously. Although the traditional businesses often bring in most of the revenue, don't neglect the 'new ones'. Give concentrated attention to your online strategy before the competition does.

47 Avoid corporate treacle

Consider all those companies where administration, processes and controls seem to dictate the daily work experience. Their original purpose and direction becomes lost, overshadowed by politics and corporate treacle. With strategic decisions often taking a minimum of nine months, many established company ideas become crushed under the weight of the corporate Goliath.

48 Old and new technologies

Start leveraging existing IT architecture to support dot com initiatives. Building a dot com architecture is a continuous process. The sooner you start the better. Although every company is unique, there are many ways dot com can be applied by your organisation. Get aligned with some technology partners and get started.

DOT COM EMPLOYEES

"Don't always depend on consensus management. Empower people to make their own decisions."
Drew Kaza, BBC

49 Match skills with staff

So how can you recruit the right people to fill all those dot com positions, when these roles did not exist a few years ago? Whether engaged in re-energising a traditional business or creating a whole new start-up, try to embrace new employment philosophies. Get all existing staff behind the dot com vision and provide dot com training for all, introduce new types of remuneration packages and flexible working practices.

50 'A' type personalities

They are 'action' orientated, they seize the opportunity and push business ahead in Internet time. Recruit this type of person and encourage them to act now.

51 Communicators

Employee communication will ensure that colleagues understand the vision to ensure they support, plan and head in the right direction with the rest of the team knowing where they are heading.

52 Insightful decision-makers

With the ever-increasing pace of change, no-one can possess all the necessary information. Therefore, you need personnel with insight and experience who act on rational intuition.

53 Curious minds

In contributing to shape this new global enterprise, you also need personnel who are constantly learning and exploring. Encourage managers to be curious and part of creating the future.

54 Flexible champions

Avoid anyone that places hierarchy over ideas. Dot coms are fluid, calling for flexible managers who can adapt teams to the latest consumer needs, competitive threats and market opportunities.

55 Portfolio workers

Recruit some people who offer their skills to you part of the time on a consultancy basis. Having a range of roles and a portfolio of jobs is the future and it's the only way you'll get the best.

56 Bold and bizarre

People with personalities build cultures. Whilst every business needs catchers, you also need some wildly creative characters who help build the complete picture and give you the edge. As Bob Head of Smile says, "Tolerate the mavericks and get them into action".

57 Be decisive

Whilst encouraging managers to make decisions, do not push power down too far. Lead by taking decisions yourself.

58 Corporate executives

Not all dot com personnel have to be whizz-kids. Experienced and respected corporate executives give strength and balance to the team, often bringing with them useful networks of contacts.

59 Dot com teams

With the right team and skills you can succeed with a small core team, the key is having strong managers in sales, marketing, content, finance and technology and also in ensuring that they work with partners to deliver results.

60 Catchers

Not everyone in the company can be an innovator. Still make certain you have some catchers who will follow through, focusing on details.

HEROIC MARKETING

"Brand will become the only differentiator."
Charles Fallon, Pets Pyjamas

61 Brand friendly URL

Choose a memorable and brand friendly URL, the shorter the better. Opt for a descriptive or intriguing name, ensuring it is extendable in terms of building the brand.

62 Get the hype

"Get the hype, get it out there and have the site ready quickly" were the wise words from Paul Barry-Walsh of NetStore. We've all seen the dot com hype. As many of the dot com heroes in this book demonstrate, this is the era of self-promotion. At last success is not a dirty word.

63 Battle of the brands

Many feared the Internet would be the death of brands, reality has shown the opposite. Brands are differentiators. Make your dot com just as distinctive and create a brand.

64 Tune in

We all have marketing formulas that we have tried and tested throughout our careers. Whether as a passion for PR, or a belief in the power of sponsorship or above-the-line advertising. However, your marketing strategy must be in tune with the dot com economy. If dot com is not embedded in your marketing strategy, then your company has yet to accept and realise that the business world has changed for the better.

65 Brand experience

The online experience is the brand, the content, the download speeds, the two-way dialogue – all adding up to create your overall brand values. Get the combination wrong and you undervalue the brand. Branding has become a dynamic part of the overall experience.

66 Use your information assets

Brands have moved away from merely delivering quality products to building long term customer loyalty. Using information, marketing must generate, evaluate and build the right relationships.

67 On and off-line integration

On and off-line campaigns should integrate as part of the marketing mix. Offer a diverse range of response options or help to educate customers so they find the online experience more enjoyable.

68 Dot com marketers

Every member of the marketing team should collaborate to develop new dot com ideas. From interactive banner advertising, email newsletters, online registration for events to delivering personalised fulfilment material over the Net, every aspect of marketing is affected.

69 Co-operative branding

Leverage your partners' brands and marketing resources. Choose partners who can help strengthen your vision and create positive brand associations. This approach accelerates your time to market and in terms of resource and time management and is also very economical.

70 Seek permission

Always seek customers' agreement before marketing to them online. Emails should have an opt in and opt out clause. This creates the right framework for future positive communication.

71 Interactive marketing

Grab attention, with interactive media like offering online quizzes or radio. Media rich marketing achieves faster results and higher click-throughs on banners.

72 Feedback counts

Positive feedback does wonders for your brand image. Yet it is a double-edged sword because the Internet enables millions of customers to share negative experiences. A group of customers with consolidated positive opinions can reinforce the brand, so develop a strong customer relationship management process.

73 Personalised attention

Reach out to customers with personalised offers and customised messages. Use the power of the technology to move direct marketing forward and build a database marketing strategy which captures information, email addresses and preferences.

74 Search engines

Take advice from Rob Wilmot of Freeserve; Marketing = Traffic. This effective marketing can begin by getting yourself listed on the right search engines.

HEROIC INFRASTRUCTURES, TECHNOLOGY FOR SUCCESS

"Continuous availability will be imperative, after all the Internet never closes."

Scott McNealy, Sun Microsystems

75 Be right first time

Technology is the backbone of the Internet age. It connects the world, provides security, communication, availability, reliability and control.

Today's Web technology is most visible when things go awry, like slow download times and impossible online ordering processes or the inability to cope with surges in demand. The key from the start is to build the right infrastructure. That can only be achieved in partnership with the right people, invest in your infrastructure from day one.

76 Technology partners

Technology is at the core of your business providing you with a competitive edge. Make sure your technology partners offer an informed view of the guiding principles to help you nurture the power of technology and avoid the pitfalls.

No one partner can deliver all the solutions you'll ever want. So work with a team of individuals that can provide the best of breed solutions.

77 Anytime, anyplace, anywhere

Your users must have flexible access to your site using any type of network enabled device. Aim for 24/7 service with no downtime periods. Your IT infrastructure must support large surges in demand, so make it scalable.

78 User security

Users must be assured of privacy, confidentiality, data integrity, virus protection and more.

79 Systems management predictability

Performance measurement is critical, anticipate problems, plan to manage your capacity and deliver.

80 Customer experience and design

Design your site from a customer perspective. Make sure it is easy to navigate, make purchase processes simple. Reward sales with loyalty programmes.

81 The outsourcing advantage

The modern Internet model provides new ways of outsourcing so you can reap the benefits of the dot com age without having to invest in building the infrastructure yourself. Outsource to experienced companies who can help enhance your expertise whilst keeping costs down.

82 The Technology advantage

Use the technology to do something better than it is being done already, wise words from John Browning.

THE QUESTION OF CASH

"Don't start it with your own money – I did that, it's incredibly stressful."

Tim Jackson, QXL

83 Venture forward

Currently, Internet-related companies claim over 60% of Venture Capitalist funding. This trend looks likely to continue. Lured by the prospect of huge stock market gains in communications, software, and dot com businesses, investors look towards Europe for new online champions. Even with the stock market fluctuations, funding is widely available for the right initiatives.

84 Profits on the horizon

Prove you can lose money and the Venture Capitalists will invest more. It shows you are ambitious – so the myth goes! In reality the key is to show growth targets. Investors and analysts want business models that scale up and grab market share. Capture customer loyalty and have competitive costs. Also, in order not to put off investors, include in the scheme eventual profit expectations.

85 Invest in market share

When should you reduce or withdraw the investment? The rule of thumb is whilst you are expanding market reach and generating future revenue streams continue to invest in building the online business. AOL and Amazon demonstrate that it takes a long time to build a real online business, Amazon is still investing and after eleven years, so is AOL.

86 Dot com bank balances

When starting a dot com enterprise think of Alexander Straub who, in less than a year, raised $40m in venture funding to launch mondus, a portal that hunts down goods and services for business customers. The average Venture Capital deals are getting bigger with a 50% increase in deals in 1999 to '98. One of the biggest published deals in 1999 was related to carsdirect.com in Los Angeles at $280m. It demonstrates if an idea is sound – the capital is available.

87   Internet stock correction

There are numerous claims of over-valued stock so be in it for the long term and remember as a sense of financial reality sets in the focus is shifting to profitability.

88   Little and large

Don't be daunted by large figures. From one perspective they illustrate that if world domination is your goal, then backed by the right business plan, support will be forthcoming, with corresponding positive responses for the smaller projects.

89   Cash is cheap

Remember money is cheap to raise. It's the expertise, branding, technology and attracting customers which are costly. Make sure you scale up your business plans to cover the expensive factors. Build a plan based on investing to out manoeuvre the competition.

90   Seducing the investors

Venture Capitalists are inundated with thousands of potential schemes. Stick to simple principles such as:

– Make sure you produce a professional business plan
– Ensure your management summary is eye-catching
– Position your ideas with clarity; simplicity sells
– Demonstrate in depth market understanding and explain your market positioning
– Outline when and how you are going to make money out of the idea
– Have an understanding of the investment schedule you require
– Highlight strong partnerships and contacts who are backing the idea
– Be visionary and show what differentiates you from others
– Employ an approachable, experienced management team
– Do not go it alone, have a strong core team to complement your skills

As Kajsa Leander from boo advises, "Write a good business plan and then continually challenge it."

91   Be well planned

"Submit a brilliant plan matched by a core team of four or five people," advises Phil Letts of Beenz. Go beyond a superficial PowerPoint presentation which many Venture Capitalists find unattractive. Peoplesound's proposal was backed with a 150-page plan that was written by a bright management team led by Ernesto Schmitt aged 29, as well as established businessmen.

92   Research

At first, 33-year-old Richard Spinks from vavo.com didn't fully appreciate the older market when he decided to set up a site for the older surfer. So he advertised for older people interested in being part of a Web project. He received 974 responses – a solid foundation that formed the basis of the amazing global community which he has built. Follow his example and back up your idea with facts.

HEROIC OPPORTUNITIES

"Hollywood wants mind control. The Internet offers an open mind."
Terry Gilliam

93   From B2C to B2B

Business-to-consumer enterprises may receive a high proportion of investment from Venture Capitalists as well as from the media hype, yet the future is in business-to-business e-commerce. It offers huge economic benefits for every business, lowering costs, improving trading efficiencies and opening up new supply lines. So start thinking B2B.

94   Cultural roadblocks

Crossing the Atlantic has not been easy. Many American sites can vouch for this. With multiple languages and culture differences, even the mighty eBay found this a challenge, with QXL having the lead over them in the UK. There is an e-invasion in Europe – so look to Europe for the future.

Possess an in-depth knowledge of the local environment, be able to strike local deals and deliver local content – it can all provide you with a head-start. The lesson is to think local then globalise.

95   Mobile e-business

According to International Data Corporation, by 2004 some 350 million people worldwide could be using the mobile Net. This extension of the Internet into hundreds of pockets, purses, and cars will produce a totally different set-up. Telephone banking is already a reality. It serves as a prelude to other services 'going mobile' including local businesses and international conglomerates.

96   Collaborations

We are witnessing a close collaboration among companies strengthening complementary brands joining to deliver unique sites. This is the powerful concept behind many of the sites from Amazon to handbag.com. The Gartner group predicts that by 2004, this will be the dominant form of e-commerce. Co-operation in the new economy invites complementary businesses to establish a cost-effective presence, broader coverage, and reduced costs.

97   Portals

Portals are emerging as important tools for targeting services to specific groups of users, including consumers and employees. The next stride is to target the business-to-business market and reduce the buying and selling complexity by offering services to related businesses as demonstrated by mondus.

98 Surfing seniors

As vavo.com demonstrates, senior citizens are proving to be a fast growing online sector. They spend more time and money online than any other group. This burgeoning senior group draws a great deal of attention with marketers who, quite against the grain, realise that the 'older' market can indeed provide valuable unsolicited ideas.

99 Seconds count

Do not just think about new ideas, think used and recycled; a whole host of opportunities are emerging for trading second-hand goods, from second-hand motor bike leathers, to selling the freight space on you lorries on the return journey back to the depot.

100 Small niche, big market

Multiply the smallest idea by the size of the Internet and you have a sustainable business model. If you get it right the whole world, not just your neighbours, are within reach.

AND FINALLY

101 Be a dot com hero NOW!!

From starting up a new dot com to adding value to Bricks & Mortar, get started now. Begin with an idea, large or small, create a business plan, set clear goals, understand the market, put customers first, work with the right partners, learn from our heroes, be passionate, take risks and break the rules.

This book is just the start. Just like the Internet, ideas are always evolving so why not visit dotcomheroes.com – it's a place to share ideas, ask questions and network.

web directory

web directory

365corp.com	Internet services for sport, entertainment sites
aisa.co.uk	Insurance and financial services
amazon.com	Online retailer, books, music, toys and more
bbc.com	Entertainment and commercial site
beenz.com	Web currency
bol.com	Books and music
boo.com	Sports and streetwear
build-online.com	Community for the construction industry
cisco.com	Internet networking solutions/routers/hubs
confetti.co.uk	Wedding portal
davidbowie.com	Artist's personal site
dell.com	Direct computer systems
egg.com	Online banking services
emigroup.com	Music and information
eventures.co.uk	Internet Venture Capitalist
everywoman.co.uk	Women's portal
excite.co.uk	Search portal with services
exodus.net	Internet services and web hosting
firsttuesday.com	Resources for new media entrepreneurs
freeserve.com	Internet Service Provider
FT.com	Global business news and services
genie.co.uk	Net-based information to cellnet mobile phones
guru.com	Connecting independent professionals
handbag.com	Portal for women
hilton.com	Virtual hotel, guest services online
internet-exchange.co.uk	Internet cafes
jungle.com	Online supermarket, from CDs to DVDs
lastminute.com	Last-minute bookings, travel, tickets
lycos.com	Search portal, providing email and services
manutd.com	Manchester United football team official site

marimba.com	Network software and managed services
mclaren.net	Official site for West McLaren Mercedes
mondus.co.uk	Procurement services for SMEs
mswebpals.org	Multiple Sclerosis portal
netimperative.com	Portal for Internet professionals
netstore.com	Internet managed services and solutions
nokia.co.uk	Mobile phones, connecting people
peoplesound.com	Download music online
petspyjamas.com	Site for pet owners
protégé.co.uk	Incubation services for Internet entrepreneurs
qxl.com	Auctions
ready2shop.com	Online shopping for women
silicon.com	Web-based TV network for IT professionals
smile.co.uk	Banking services
sojewish.com	Jewish community portal
sportal.com	Sports portal
sun.com	Hardware, software, services that power the Net
tate.org.uk	World leading arts, Tate modern and Tate Britain
teamphilips.com	Site of, international yachtsman, Pete Goss
telegraph.co.uk	Daily Telegraph website
theplanet.net	Internet Service Provider
thinknatural.com	Natural healthcare products and information
upmystreet.com	Local information services
vavo.com	Portal for the over 45's
victorchandler.com	Online betting
virgin.com	Portal for Virgin's multi-faceted businesses
virginbiz.net	Internet services/support for SMEs

special thanks

We're the dot in .com™

Sun has helped more than 500,000 companies around the world address the opportunities of the dot com world. They have delivered solutions to many of the companies in this book. Together Sun and strategic partners provide highly reliable, scalable hardware and software platforms and solutions for the dot com age. They are the dot in .com.

For more information please visit sun.co.uk or sun.com

A special campaign for the Year 2000, initiated by ITV and sponsored by companies including Freeserve and BP, the Year of Promise encourages people and companies to make a simple, positive commitment for the year ahead in a free, national register. From promising to give blood regularly to helping the homeless, the Year of Promise is already helping to make the world – and the new Millennium – a better place. Our promise is to support community related Internet projects through the royalties gained from this book.

Gyro is the one agency that truly understands the changing marketing communications needs of technology companies and dot coms. Whether driving worldwide programmes for the best known technology companies or assisting the launch of new ones, Gyro combines a unique blend of strategic planning with the most creative ideas. Based in London and San Francisco, Gyro has more than a fair share of its own marketing heroes and has supported this project through friendship and a shared passion for the Internet.

For more information please visit gyro.co.uk or email richard_perry@gyro.co.uk

dot com glossary

dot com glossary

Auction
An electronic market, which can exist in both a business-to-business and business-to-consumer context. Sellers offer products or services to buyers through a website with a structured process for price setting and fulfilment. Web auctions may follow English, Dutch, reverse-bid or sealed-bid processes.

Availability
Availability is a measure of your computing "uptime" measured in percentages. Ensuring high availability requires all elements of a computing system to work well. In mission-critical applications high availability can be achieved through clustering where if one system fails another can take over.

Backbone
The primary communication mechanism of a distributed system rather like the motorways of a road system. At the local level, a backbone is a line or set of lines that local area networks connect to for a wide area network connection or within a local area network to span distances efficiently (for example, between buildings). On the Internet or other wide area network, a backbone is a set of paths that local or regional networks connect to for long-distance interconnection.

Bandwidth
The bandwidth of a transmitted communications signal is a measure of the range of frequencies the signal occupies. Generally speaking, bandwidth is proportional to the complexity of the data being sent across the network. For example, it takes more bandwidth to download a picture file in one second than it takes to download a page of text in one second. Large sound files, computer programs, and animated videos require a great deal of bandwidth, and can sometimes cause the system to slow down in performance.

Banners
A banner can either be an image that announces the name or identity of a site (and often is spread across the width of the Web page) or is an advertising image. Advertisers sometimes count banner "views," or the number of times a banner graphic image was downloaded over a period of time.

Brick and Mortar
Describes a traditional company with non-Web channels as the sales outlet for its products or services. As opposed to Clicks & Mortar which uses Web channels as the sales outlet.

Browser
A software program used to locate and display information on an intranet, extranet or the Internet.

Business-to-business commerce (B2B)
Using electronic interactions to conduct business among enterprises, typically as a result of formal, contractual arrangements. B2B functions include sophisticated Web authorisation and control (WAC) for delivery of sensitive price, contract and content information for each partner; catalogues that provide custom views based on access control and parametric search for serious business buyers; and order entry functions such as standardised 'ship to' locations, dynamic order re-calculation and payment options.

Business-to-consumer commerce (B2C)

Using electronic interactions to conduct business with consumers. B2C may include formal relationships (e.g. customers with assets under care or with subscription services or content) and ad hoc relationships (formed in real time to enable a new user to buy, sell or access information).

Buy side

Processes for companies to purchase products. Includes requisitioning, product catalogues, approvals, user identification, purchase order creation, payment processing and integration to other systems.

.com

When these letters appear in the last part of a URL, it indicates that the host computer is run by a commercial organisation (often in the United States). There are a variety of different top level 'domain' types in addition to .com, typically .co.uk (UK company), .org (organisation), .ac (academic) and .gov (government). The very phrase dot com has now been widely accepted as a generic term for the Internet.

Content provider

A firm whose products are information-based (content), including services to access and manage the content.

Cookie

A cookie is information that a website puts on your hard disk so that it can remember something about you at a later time. Cookies are able to record likes, dislikes and preferences so that it can present a user with information and offers specific to the individual user. Cookies create great opportunities for advertisers and direct marketers, Web users must agree to let cookies be saved for them but, in general, it helps websites to serve users better.

Customer Relationship Management (CRM)

A technology-enabled strategy to convert data-driven decisions into business actions in response to, and in anticipation of, actual customer behaviour. From a technology perspective, CRM represents the systems and infrastructure required to capture, analyse and share all facets of the customer's relationship with the enterprise. From a strategy perspective, it represents a process to measure and allocate organisational resources to those activities that have the greatest return and impact on profitable customer relationships.

Datacentre

The datacentre is the repository of all information and should allow mainframe predictability but with (controlled) connectivity to users who need information.

Datamining

Datamining is the analysis of data for relationships that have not previously been discovered. For example, the analysis of sales records for a particular brand of car might, if sufficiently correlated and related to other market data, reveal a predisposition by the same parties to the purchase of golf equipment.

Data warehousing

A data warehouse is a centralised storage area for all or significant parts of the data that an enterprise's various business systems collect.

Digital

This is the electronic technology that generates, stores, and processes data in two states: positive and non-positive. Positive is expressed by the number 1 and non-positive by the number 0 (binary). Thus, data transmitted or stored with digital technology is expressed as a string of 0s and 1s. Each of these state digits is referred to as a bit. Prior to digital technology, electronic transmission was limited to analogue technology, which conveys data as electronic signals of varying frequency or amplitude that are added to carrier waves of a given frequency. Broadcast and telephone transmission has conventionally used analogue technology.

Domain

Domains are the Internet's method of allocating a place in the naming hierarchy to Internet server sites. An Internet domain name consists of a sequence of names (labels) separated by periods (dots) i.e. www.sun.com.

Domain Name System (DNS)

The domain name system (DNS) is the way that Internet domain names are located and translated into IP (Internet Protocol) addresses. A domain name is a meaningful and easy-to-remember 'handle' for an Internet address. Because maintaining a central list of domain name/IP address correspondences would be impractical, the lists of domain names and IP addresses are distributed throughout the Internet in a hierarchy of authority.

Downtime

A measure of the amount of time the system is not available for use, downtime can be planned (for example during maintenance) or unplanned due to a system problem or failure. Unlike uptime, downtime is measured in physical time rather than as a percentage.

E-25

Directory of the top 25 Internet start-ups.

E-business

Involves the complete transformation of business processes, distribution channels and organisation structures to create a high-performance company that uses Internet technology.

E-commerce (EC)

Electronic commerce is the use of communication technologies to transmit business information and transact business. Taking an order over the telephone is a simple form of EC. Internet commerce is also EC, but is only one of several advanced forms of EC that use technology, integrated applications and business processes to link enterprises. Simplistically, it means doing business from a website, however, it leads to the extension of your supply chain, and may create significant cost savings in the business.

E-market maker

Intermediaries that develop a B2B e-marketplace of buyers and sellers within an industry, geographic region or affinity group. They enter supply chains introducing new efficiencies and new ways of selling and purchasing products and services by providing content, value-added services, and often e-commerce capabilities. A third party within a trading community generally manages them.

E-marketplace

A website that enables buyers to select from many suppliers. E-marketplaces – which focus on putting the buyer in control – are buying environments that aggregate supplier content and provide decision support tools that enable a buyer to make the most informed decision.

Encryption

The conversion of data into a form, called a cipher, that cannot be easily understood by unauthorised people. Decryption is the process of converting encrypted data back into its original form, so it can be understood by the recipient.

E-procurement

E-procurement is the business-to-business purchase and sale of supplies and services over the Internet. An important part of many B2B sites, e-procurement websites allow qualified and registered users to look for buyers or sellers of goods and services. Depending on the approach, buyers or sellers may specify prices or invite bids. Transactions can be initiated and completed. Ongoing purchases may qualify customers for volume discounts or special offers. Pioneers of e-procurement include Ford, GM and Daimler Chrysler.

Enterprise Resource Planning (ERP)

The process of integrating personnel, sales, manufacturing and financial functions into a single unified system.

Extranet

A collaborative, Internet-based network to link an enterprise with its suppliers, customers or other external business partners and to facilitate intercompany relationships. Extranets use Internet-derived applications and technology to become the secured extensions of internal business processes to external business partners.

Firewall

A system that connects a local network to the Internet but acts as a security perimeter between internal and external data or systems.

Graphical User Interface (GUI)

An aid to programming which negates the need for sophisticated programming skills. A good example of a GUI is an Internet browser such as Netscape.

Heritage/legacy applications

Those that have been inherited from languages, platforms, and techniques earlier than current technology. Most enterprises who use computers have legacy applications and databases that serve critical business needs. The challenge is to keep the legacy application running while converting to new technology.

Homepage

The entry page of a website usually the main page of a company, organisation or person.

Host

The primary computer in a multiple computer installation/network.

Hypertext Mark-up Language (HTML)

The basic programming language of the Web. HTML is a file format for hypertext documents on the Internet. It is very simple and allows for the embedding of images, sounds, video streams, form fields and simple text formatting.

Intelligent agent

Software that acts as an intermediary for a person by performing some activity. Agents can "learn" an individual's preferences and act in the person's best interest and may even negotiate and complete transactions. A purchasing manager's agent may learn corporate specifications, determine when inventory is low and search the Internet for the lowest-cost supplier.

Internet

The Internet is in essence a huge network of computers, where any one computer can, if given permission, get information from any other computer. Sometimes referred to as the Net, the Internet is the biggest network in the world. The most widely used part of the Internet is the World Wide Web, where users can gain access to millions of pages of information throughout the globe. The primary factor that distinguishes the Internet from telecommunications networks is its use of protocols called TCP/IP (Transmission Control Protocol/Internet Protocol). Two recent adaptations of Internet technology, the intranet and the extranet, also make use of the TCP/IP protocol.

Internet Sales Outlet (ISO)

A third-party website that attracts visitors looking to buy goods or services. ISOs make money by selling links or ads that lead directly to the merchant websites, or by selling products or services on behalf of Web merchants.

Intranet

An internal corporate version of the Internet that runs via Internet protocols and tools.

ISDN

(Integrated Subscriber Digital Network) 2 X 64kbs over standard POTS copper loop, can aggregate both lines to give 128kbs.

ISP/ASP/FSP/CSP

Short for Internet Service Provider, Application Service Provider, Full Service Provider and Commerce Service Provider. An ISP is a company that provides access to the Internet. For a monthly fee, the service provider gives you a software package, username, password and access phone number. Equipped with a modem, you can then log on to the Internet and browse the World Wide Web and USENET, and send and receive email. In addition to serving individuals, ISPs also serve large companies, providing a direct connection from the company's networks to the Internet. ISPs themselves are connected to one another through Network Access Points (NAPs). ISPs are also called IAPs (Internet Access Providers).

ASP

An ASP is a company that hosts and manages business applications on behalf of a client. These applications can range from basic email to groupware and data mart applications to extremely complex and demanding applications such as Enterprise Resource Planning (ERP) and Customer Relationship Management (CRM).

The value proposition of the ASP is very compelling: take advantage of the ASP's expertise and economies of scale in managing applications, and avoid the pain and expense of hiring your own specialists and constantly installing, maintaining, and upgrading packaged software. With ASPs, you can have top-tier business systems right away for a predictable monthly fee.

FSP
Full Service Provider. Takes the ASP model further – by offering full business process 'outsourcing'. Can be viewed as traditional 'bureau service'.

CSP
Service providers that specialise in Web-enabled e-commerce services, as well as those offering specific software or outsourcing support for these services.

Java
An object-oriented programming language which allows different computers to communicate with each other across networks.

Jini
'Spontaneous networking'. Using the Jini architecture, will mean that users will be able to plug refrigerators, computers, storage devices, speakers, in fact any kind of device directly into a network and every other computer, device, and user on the network will know that the new device has been added and is available. Each pluggable device will define itself immediately to a network device, and can seamlessly communicate with all other devices on the network.

Knowledge Management (KM)
A business process that formalises management and leverage of a firm's intellectual assets. KM is an enterprise discipline that promotes a collaborative and integrative approach to the creation, capture, organisation, access and use of information assets, including the tacit, uncaptured knowledge of people.

Lead-time
The lead-time of a product is the amount of time it takes for a product to be delivered from the inception of the original order. The pressure is always on to reduce lead-times, particularly with the speed of ordering created by the Internet.

Leased line
A leased line is a telephone line that has been leased for private use. In some contexts, it's called a dedicated line. A leased line is usually contrasted with a switched line or dial-up line.

Market spoilers or market killers
Web-based businesses that aggregate information about a market and its suppliers, present the aggregated information to consumers via a website, and increasingly offer decision support to allow customers to differentiate based on independent validation of competitors' services and features. These businesses diminish the advantage of suppliers that compete through brand identity or reputation.

M-commerce
Mobile commerce, is the act of using a mobile device to transact over the Internet.

Mission critical

Typically a mission critical application is an application which for operational reasons cannot be allowed to fail. An example of a mission critical system is a banks payment system where any failure would cause massive financial damage to the organisation.

Modem (Modulator-Demodulator)

A modem converts digital language from a device such as a computer into analogue signals for transmission across the telephone network, and then demodulates the incoming analogue signal converting it back into a signal for the digital device.

Networks (LAN & WAN)

Local Area Network (LAN)
A small network of computers which operate 'within the fence' i.e. with no external access via the Internet/leased line.
Wide Area Network (WAN)
A network that connects users together with no constraints over location using either leased lines or the Internet to connect many LANs together. Ideal for companies with several different locations.

Operating system

An operating system (sometimes abbreviated as 'OS' is the program that, after being initially loaded into the computer manages all the other programs in a computer. The other programs are called applications. The applications make use of the operating system by making requests for services through a defined application program interface (API). In addition, users can interact directly with the operating system through an interface such as a command language. Examples of operating systems are Solaris and Windows.

Outsourcing

Outsourcing is an arrangement in which one company provides services for another company that could have been provided in-house. Outsourcing is a trend that is becoming more common in information technology, in particular in the field of application provision, for example email.

Personal Digital Assistant (PDA)

A term for any small mobile hand-held device that provides computing and information storage and retrieval capabilities for personal or business use. Most PDAs allow Internet access.

Personalisation

Using continually adjusted user profiles to match content or services to individuals. Personalisation includes determining a user's interest based on his or her preferences or behaviour, constructing business rules to select relevant content based on those preferences or behaviours, and presenting the content to the user in an integrated, cohesive format.

Portal

A high-traffic, broadly appealing website with a wide range of content, services and vendor links. It acts as a value-added middleman by selecting the content sources and assembling them together in a simple-to-navigate (and customise) interface for presentation to the end user. Portals typically include services such as email, community and chat.

Protocols

A formal description of messages to be exchanged and rules to be followed for two or more systems to exchange information.

File Transfer Protocol (FTP)
A standard Internet protocol, it is the simplest way to exchange files between computers on the Internet.
HTTP (Hypertext Transfer Protocol)
The Hypertext Transfer Protocol (HTTP) is the set of rules for exchanging files (text, graphic images, sound, video, and other multimedia files) on the World Wide Web. HTTP is an application protocol.
TCP-IP (Transport Control Protocol/Internet Protocol)
The default protocol suite originally developed for the Internet.

Scalability

The ability of your systems to grow with a company's needs and expected utilisation.

Sell side

Processes for companies to sell their products, including catalogues, transaction processors, payment processors, and supply chain management methods and tools.

Server system

A system that supplies services to other computers (clients) on a network.

Service provider

As companies of all sizes start to use the Internet, outsourcing is gaining in credibility – and popularity. Service providers provide the vital link between the enterprise and the opportunities the Internet creates. Service providers will host a company's software applications, email and Internet connections leaving the company to concentrate on their own core business skills.

Supply Chain Management (SCM)

The process of optimising delivery of goods, services and information from supplier to customer. SCM is a set of business processes that encompass a trading-partner community engaged in a common goal of satisfying the end customer.

Uptime

Measure of the time the computer system is running and available for use.

URL (Uniform Resource Locator)

The URL is the address of a file (resource) accessible on the Internet. For example http//www.sun.com is a URL.

Value chain

An analysis of where in the supply chain the company can add value to the customer. This analysis is vital in maximising the possibility of success in any e-commerce operation.

Wireless Application Protocol (WAP)

The Wireless Application Protocol is a secure specification that allows users to access information instantly via handheld wireless devices such as mobile phones, pagers, two-way radios, smartphones and communicators. It defines a connection protocol and markup language, similar to a reduced version of HTML based upon XML and delivered by a microbrowser.